I Know The Best Of Mankind!

OUR NOBLEST PROPHET MUHAMMAD

By

Al Hakim Al Misry PhD.

Table of content

INTRODUCTION

For a long time, a need was felt for a brief book that captured the essence of the way of life and teachings of the Prophet Muhammad, and at the same time served as an easy introduction for the layperson to the greatest personality that mankind has ever known. Despite many reference and scholarly books on the subject, only a few give a glimpse of the magnificent character and conduct of the final messenger of Allah in the way that the work of Al Hakim Al Misry do.

The life and teachings of the Prophet were central and omnipresent to the many books written by this author , where he extensively referred to the Prophet's teachings or his policies, citing the stance that the Prophet maintained in various events, or the policies he had adopted with respect to particular issues. He based his analyses on the teachings of the Prophet Muhammad may Allah bless him and his impeccable family.

This work is not intended to be a comprehensive chronological presentation of the life of the Prophet, nor does it aim to detail all his teachings. It is intended to give some idea about the historic transformation initiated by the Prophet and the change he induced in the course of mankind's life.

To help appreciate the significance of the universal renaissance that the Prophet Muhammad began some fourteen centuries ago, it is necessary to be aware of the status quo that prevailed at the time prior to start of his prophetic mission, even if outlined very briefly. As an eyewitness of the state of affair of the human society at the time, Imam Ali says:

"Allah sent Muhammad sometime after the other messengers, and after the nations of the world had been slumbering for a long time. Strife had become entrenched, affairs disparate, and wars raging. The light of the world had become obscured, and vanities had become foremost. The leaves of life had then become yellow, its fruits rare, and its water dried up. The lighthouse of guidance had crumbled, and the signs of ruin had become manifest. The world scowled upon its people, frowned in the face of those who sought after it. Strife was the only fruit, carrion the only food, fear the only motto, the sword the only clothing."

In another speech Imam Ali describes the "Age of Ignorance"that prevailed before the prophetic mission:

"Allah sent Muhammad when the people were astray and in confusion, lost in strife. Their vain desires had overcome them, and arrogance had brought them down. The ignorance of the times had made them make light of the ignorant ones. They were helpless, caught in the earthquake and calamity of ignorance. So Muhammad went to great lengths to give wise counsel and walked the right path and called to wisdom and fine preaching."

It was with this kind of background that the Prophet of Islam began his mission to teach and educate the masses, to promote virtue and prohibit vice; to encourage them to reflect upon and therefore reform their state of affairs and determine their destiny.

This work is a small presentation of events in which the prophet was involved, to help reflect on the supreme personality that has left its mark on the course of humanity, and it shall continue to do so for as long as man lives on this planet.

On some occasions in this work some of the events may be similar or the same, this is because it was decided that the chapters that were taken from the various books by the author remain intact as much as possible and with minimum alteration, although some minor editing were made.

In the majority of cases the events are cited without much or any comments or analysis. This is due to a number of reasons:

- To keep this work as short and brief as possible, and not lengthy and tiresome;

- To allow the reader to draw his/her own conclusion(s), which in most cases are self- explanatory. Even the quotes from western intellectuals that have been cited by the editorial board have been placed towards the end of the book, so that these may not influence the mind of the reader prior to reading this work.

The book is comprised of six chapters. Chapters Two to
Five are outlines the qualities of the Noble Prophet.
Chapter One presents glimpse of the biography of the
Prophet Muhammad. This part was included to give the
reader a glimpse of the life of the Prophet from his birth
up to his death.

Chapter Two addresses some of the moral qualities and
values of the Prophet; whether in their outward
manifestation such as his interactions with others be it
friends, foes, or even animals, or in innate and personal
virtues such as his humility, abstinence, steadfastness,
bravery, and prayers.

Chapter Three outlines the general policies and stances
that the Prophet took at times of conflict. It addresses the
etiquettes and strategies the Prophet adopted for battle,
his efforts to avoid fighting by giving his opponents the
choice of war or peace, his tolerance towards his
opponents and his forgiveness of traitors, his teachings
on the treatment of prisoners and the prohibition of
torture, his conduct upon victory, and finally his position
in the eyes of his foes.

Chapter Four sheds some light on the Prophet's social
policies as well as his personal conduct mostly when the
Islamic community took hold in the city of Medina. The
Prophet continued to win hearts and minds of the public
through his social and fiscal policies.

Chapter Five presents various teachings and sayings of
the Prophet Muhammad on a variety of ethical and

social issues that signify the characteristics of an Islamic society. Such teachings, which in general address every aspect of life in this world, and also matters concerning the hereafter, are traditionally referred to as the hadith of the Prophet, and the conduct of the Prophet, and the manifestation of those teachings - known as Sunnah - are adhered to by the devotees.

Chapter Six is a selection of statements by western thinkers about the Prophet Muhammad.

The significance of this book lies in the fact it presents the role model to humanity in the person of the Prophet Muhammad who gave the best possible that can be given and sacrificed with all he had in order to guide humanity to the path that guarantees prosperity for it in this world and in the hereafter, and indeed he succeeded in doing so in the best possible manner.

It is therefore not unexpected when non-Muslim intellectuals consider him to be the most influential person in the history of mankind, as the American scholar Michael H. Hart states in his work "The 100: A Ranking of the Most Influential Persons in History":

Muhammad was the only man in history who was supremely successful on both the religious and secular levels.

The writer George Bernard-Shaw says:

I hold the religion of Muhammad in the highest esteem
for its astounding vitality. It seems to me to be the only
religion which is equipped to suit the changing faces of
life and which is appropriate for all ages. I have studied
the life of this amazing man and I believe that he
deserves to be called the savior of the human race.

And thus the prophet not only deserves to be a role
model for humanity, but in fact he is the best role model
mankind can ever find. The Almighty states in the
Qur'an,

Ye have indeed in the Messenger of Allah an excellent
example. (33:21).
Addressing the Prophet himself, the Almighty states:

And indeed you have sublime ethics.

And finally Imam Ali peace be upon him declares,
"Whoever seeks a role model, let the Prophet be his role
model; otherwise, he shall have no safeguard against
perdition."

Chapter 1:
A Brief Biography Of Prophet Muhammad

We have sent thee not except as a mercy to all the Worlds. (The Holy Qur'an, The Prophets, 21:107). We have sent thee not except as a giver of glad-tidings and a warner to all the peoples. (The Holy Qur'an, Sheba, 34:28).

****

Muhammad was son of Abdullah, who was son of Abdul-Muttalib, who was son of Hashim - whose ancestry reached the Prophet Ismael son of the Prophet Abraham, peace be upon them.

The Prophet Muhammad was born in the city of Mecca, in Arabia, on a Friday, the 17th day of the lunar month of Rabi-I, in the year 570 CE into a noble family whose fathers and ancestors were amongst the chiefs of the Quraysh tribe, and the Bani-Hashim clan. His Prophetic mission began on the 27th day of the month of Rajab, in the year 610 CE, when he received the first divine revelation. Then the Qur'an was revealed to the Prophet progressively according to the circumstances of the time over a period of 23 years.

The Prophet Muhammad died on the 28th day of the month of Safar in the 11th year of the Hijrah 1, 630 CE.

His Childhood

Muhammad's father Abdullah son of Abdul-Muttalib was the best and most pious among the sons of Abdul-Muttalib and his most beloved. Abdullah died while Muhammad was still in his mother's womb. All that he left behind were five camels and a servant girl named Barakah, also known as Umm Ayman, who was Muhammad's nanny.

Abdullah was a true believer and a monotheist. After his death, Muhammad's grandfather, Abdul- Muttalib, became his guardian. Abdul-Muttalib was one of the chieftains of the tribe of Quraysh, and a believer in Allah (in the way of Prophet Abraham), as was Abu Talib, a brother of Abdullah. Abdul-Muttalib always respected and honored treaties and adopted the finest of morals. He loved the poor and helped pilgrims. He would even feed the wild beasts and the birds of the mountaintops. He would feed people in times of famine and would restrain wrongdoers.

Muhammad's mother was Aminah, daughter of Wahab son of Abd Manaf, son of Kilab. She was also a believer in Allah. When Muhammad was born his mother said: "As soon as I put my child on the ground he leaned with his hands on the ground, raised his head to the skies and looked at the horizons all the while speaking in phrases of monotheism. Then a voice called out to me saying:

'The best of mankind has been born, so name him
Muhammad.'"

Then Aminah sent for Abdul-Muttalib. He came to her
and she said: 'A wondrous boy has been born to your
family.' Then she brought baby Muhammad to him.
Abdul-Muttalib looked at him and entered the Kabah2
and prayed to Allah. He, then left the Kabah and
returning the infant to his mother and named him
Muhammad.
Muhammad was not even seven years old when his
mother died. After his mother's death, his grandfather
Abdul-Muttalib assumed his guardianship. Because of
his knowledge of the status of the child and his faith in
him, Abdul-Muttalib treated Muhammad with more care
and attention than his other children.
A group of the Medlaj Clan came to Mecca and when
they saw Muhammad they said to his grandfather: 'Take
good care of him for we have never seen another of his
station.' Abdul-Muttalib told this to Abu Talib in his will
and asked him to heed what they had said and take care
of him. Muhammad was eight when his grandfather
died, and he was taken into the care of his uncle Abu
Talib.
Abu Talib, chief of the Bani-Hashim clan within the
Quraysh then became the guardian of Muhammad from
his eighth year. Abu Talib went on to protect and serve
the Messenger of Allah, defending him and honoring
him throughout the testing times of his Prophethood,
until the last breath of his life.

His Adulthood

Muhammad grew up to become a fine young man. He became known for his excellent manners, and because of the honesty in his conduct and dealings he was referred to as al- Sadiq (The Truthful One) and al-Amin (The Trustworthy One).

As a youngster Muhammad used to accompany his uncle on his business trips to Syria. When the Messenger of Allah reached the age of twelve he journeyed with his uncle Abu Talib as far as Basra. A Christian monk, named George, saw him there and recognized him by his description. He took his hand and said: "This is the chief of the Worlds, God has send him as a mercy to the Worlds."Abu Talib asked: "How do you know this?"He said: "We find him mentioned in our books."He asked Abu Talib to take him back fearing for his safety.

As an adult, Muhammad worked as a trader between the cities of Mecca and Damascus, and earned a great reputation in the process. Having heard of the reputation of Muhammad, Lady Khadijah, one of the noblest of the Quraysh, on one occasion commissioned him to take charge of some of her trading business between the two cities.

Lady Khadijah sent one of her servants, Maysarah, along with him to keep an eye on him and report back to her. Having seen his performance in the business, and the

returns he brought, as well as his honesty, Lady
Khadijah put Muhammad in charge of her business.

Although she had many proposals of marriage from
various dignitaries of the Quraysh, Lady Khadijah
declined them all. It is reported that it was Lady
Khadijah who, albeit indirectly and discreetly, made the
marriage proposal to Muhammad. Some historians have
reported that when they married in 595 CE they were
both 25 years old.

Lady Khadijah gave birth to seven children. All of the
Prophet's children were from Khadijah. The male
children who were all born in Mecca were: Al-Qasim,
which is where Muhammad's epithet (Abul-Qasim;
meaning Qasim's father),Ibrahim(Which was named
after prophet Ibrahim) and Abdullah(meaning the
servant of Allah). The boys all died young during the
lifetime of the Prophet.

His daughters were Fatimah, who married Imam Ali son
of Abu Talib, and bore him Imam Hasan and Imam
Husayn. Zaynab and Ruqqoyah who after the death of
each other married Uthman the third caliph after
Muhammed's death. And ummul khulthum. Fatimah was
the only one of the siblings to survive the Messenger of
Allah. The Prophet Muhammad used to say Hasan and
Husayn are two Imams (leaders) whether they rise up
(against tyranny) or not.

Ali was born to Abu Talib and his wife Fatimah bint
Asad in 600 CE. Ali's birth was associated with a

particularly significant phenomenon. When Fatimah bint Asad was in labor she came to the Kabah pleading to God for help with her labor. It is reported by various narrators and recorded by many chroniclers that as she was engaged in her prayers by the southern wall of the Kabah, the wall split open and she entered the House, whereby the wall returned to its normal state.

Having observed this extraordinary phenomenon, people who were present tried to follow her into the House through the opening but did not succeed. They then tried to go inside the House through its door but could not unlock the door. Reports indicate that she was inside the House for three days, and when she left the House with her newborn she did so in the same manner as she had entered the House.

The Prophet Muhammad took particular interest in baby Ali, and he played a major role in Ali's upbringing and education. Ali would be the most ardent supporter of the Prophet throughout the difficult years of his mission to convey the divine message and the teachings of Islam to the masses.

Start Of His Mission

The Prophet Muhammad used to spend much time in prayer and worship of the one God. This he used to do in a cave, known as Hira, in the al-Noor mountain near the city of Mecca.

In 610 CE, at the age of forty, Muhammad received the
first of the divine revelations when he was engaged in
devotion and prayer inside the cave of Hira:

In the name of Allah the Merciful, the Compassionate;
Read in the name of thy Lord who created, Created man
from a clot, Read and thy lord is the most noble, Who
taught by pen, Taught man what he knew not ... (96:1-5).
The Prophet Muhammad conveyed the news and the
Message to Ali and Lady Khadijah. Ali and Lady
Khadijah both embraced the new revelation instantly and
without any hesitation.

Khadijah was thus the first woman to believe in the
Messenger of Allah and the first woman to pray with
him. She supported him wholeheartedly and spent all her
wealth in the way of Allah. She was the first woman that
the Prophet married and he married no other during her
lifetime. She was immensely loyal to the Prophet. The
Angel Gabriel ordered him to convey a special greeting
and a blessing from God and ordered that he gave the
land of Fadak to Fatimah as an appreciation for what her
mother had spent in the way of Allah.

The Prophet Muhammad began to invite individuals to
the new revelation, albeit in secret. There were very few
supporters and believers. When the Prophet performed a
congregational prayer, he was joined by were Lady
Khadijah and Ali. This low-key approach continued for
three years.

Afterwards, on instructions from the Almighty, the Prophet's invitation to Islam started to became more and more public. The Almighty instructed His messenger to begin with his clan:

And warn your nearest kinsmen (26:214).
For this purpose the Prophet Muhammad prepared a banquet and invited the elders and chiefs of the Bani-Hashim, who were forty in number. After they were served with a good feast, the Prophet invited them to Islam. He called upon them to support him in his mission, and promised them that whoever did so would be appointed as his successor.

Yet, none took up the offer dismissing the Prophet and his mission as nonsense, with the sole exception of Ali. Ridiculing the whole thing, the Bani Hashim chiefs turned to Abu Talib saying, "Your son will be your commander, you should obey him!"Nevertheless the mission continued unabated albeit with very few supporters.

Resonance Of His Call

The followers of the new religion started to grow, and so did the concern of the Quraysh towards them. The elders of Quraysh send Abu Talib, the trusted uncle of the Prophet to him, asking him to stop his call for this new religion, and in return they would give him whatever he wanted. "If you want wealth, we will give you as much as you want, if you want women we will marry you the

most beautiful women of Arabia, and if you want
position and status we will make you the owner-king
over us."

When Abu Talib conveyed the message of the elders of
Quraysh to his nephew-prophet, the Messenger of Allah
replied, "I swear by the Almighty that if they put the Sun
in my right hand and the Moon in my left on condition
so that I desist from this affair I would not leave it until
Allah causes it to prevail or I die in the process."Then
the Messenger of Allah began to weep and rose and
made to leave, but Abu Talib called him and said:
"Come back my nephew. Say what you like my nephew,
for by Allah I will never hand you over to them ever."

The Quraysh realized that they were dealing with a true
and determined prophet. From then on, open hostility
towards this new religion, its prophet, and its followers
started to increase. Lady Khadijah dedicated all her
wealth and resources for the cause of her prophet-
husband's mission. The extent of this hostility reached
blatant persecution of the followers of the new religion
and its prophet.

'Neutralise The Messenger And His Message'

Then the Quraysh plotted amongst themselves about the
companions of the Messenger of Allah who had entered
Islam with him from amongst their tribes. Each tribe
pounced upon any of its own who were Muslims,
tormented them and forced them out from their religion.

Abu Talib protected the Messenger of Allah, and seeing what the Quraysh were doing to the sons of Hashim and Abdul-Muttalib, he called upon them to protect the Messenger of Allah just as he was protecting him. So they gathered with him and stood up with him, except for Abu Talib's brother Abu Lahab and his sons wife who had assisted the Quraysh against the Prophet.

Then the Quraysh openly decided to kill the Messenger of Allah. When this news reached Abu Talib he gathered the sons of Hashim and Abdul-Muttalib and took the Messenger of Allah to his quarter and protected him from those who sought to kill him.

The Quraysh imposed total and complete embargo against the Prophet and his followers in all its forms; social, economic, political, etc. No citizen of Mecca was allowed to buy from or sell to them, no one was allowed to marry anyone of them, or even befriend or socialize with them, not even help them. Nor would a peace settlement be accepted from them ever, nor they would be shown any mercy until they had handed over the Messenger of Allah to be killed.

The Quraysh agreed to draw up a document to this effect, and one of them wrote this document in his own hand, which subsequently was afflicted by paralysis, and then they hung the document inside the Kabah.

The Prophet and many of his followers, and members of the Hashim clan withdrew to Abu Talib and entered the

Abu Talib's Quarter known as Sheb Abu Talib, which had become their virtual open-top prison. Their condition deteriorated as time went by, and although some friends of sympathizers managed to smuggle in some help to the Muslims, but this was few and far between. There they remained in the quarter for three years until they were exhausted. The voices of the children could be heard from the quarter crying of hunger.

The Quraysh also increased the pressure on those who had entered Islam but had not entered the quarter. The trials became grave and the Muslims were severely shaken. It is reported that Ali son of Abu Talib used to secretly leave the quarter in disguise and fetch foodstuff to the besieged, carrying it into the quarter on his back.

In one of the divine revelations made to him, the Messenger of Allah informed his uncle Abu Talib that Allah had sent woodworms to their document that had eaten every word except the name of Allah. Having heard this Abu Talib said: "No! By the falling stars, you have not lied to me."

Abu Talib set out with a group of the clan of Abdul-Muttalib until he reached the vicinity of the Kabah, which was full of the people of Quraysh. He spoke and said to them:

"Something has occurred which may be a cause for a settlement between you and us so bring out your document. They said: 'The time has come for you to accept and recant. Only one man has caused the split between you and us, and you have put your people in jeopardy because of him.'

Abu Talib said: "I propose a matter for you in which there is fairness. My nephew has told me and he has not lied to me, that Allah distances Himself from this document and has erased all your treachery and enmity and all that remains written is His name. If it is as he has said then by Allah, we will never hand him over to you until the last of us dies. If what he has said is false then we will hand him over to you so that you may kill him or spare him as you wish.'

They said: "We agree."Then they opened the document and found it as they had been told but some of them clung to their falsehood and obstinacy and said: "This is sorcery from your companion."Then some of those who had made the pact spoke and tore up the document.

End Of One Torment And Start Of Others.

The clan of Hashim then felt safe enough to emerge from their quarter and once more mingle with the people. This was in the tenth year of the noble prophethood, circa 620 CE.

It was less than six months after the end of this trial when Abu Talib passed away. Then the Prophet's wife

Lady Khadijah also died only three days after Abu Talib according to some accounts. The Messenger of Allah was very saddened and named this year the 'Year of Sorrow'.

The loss of Abu Talib and Lady Khadijah dealt a severe blow to the Prophet at a time when he needed these two most. The death of Abu Talib cleared the last hurdle for the Quraysh, and if the presence of Abu Talib imposed certain limits and drew some red lines for the Quraysh that they could not cross, now his death left them free to do to the Prophet what was the unthinkable while Abu Talib was alive.

With the death of Abu Talib, the trials meted out by his tribe to the Messenger of Allah grew more barbaric and audacious. Once when the Prophet was praying by the Kabah, one of the idolaters approached and violently tried to strangle him.

The Quraysh encouraged the foolish to throw dirt on the Prophet's face and head. They used to throw filth, blood and thorns at his door. Ummayah ibn Khalaf used to insult the Prophet until his face became red but still the Prophet would not say anything to him. When a fool threw the dirt in the face of the Messenger of Allah, he entered his house with the dirt still on his head. Fatimah began to clean the dirt from his head. She was crying and the Messenger of Allah saying: "Do not cry my daughter, for Allah will protect your father."He also said: "The Quraysh could not harm me until Abu Talib died."

It is related from Khabab who said: 'I approached the Prophet when he was reclining in the shade of the Kabah. This was after we had received some harm from the Polytheists. I said to him: "O Messenger of Allah, will you not invoke Allah?"He sat up red in face and said: "Among those who came before you, there were those whose skins would be scraped off with combs of iron down to the bone and this did not divert them from their religion. Allah will complete this matter until a rider may travel from Sana to Hadralmaut with nothing to fear but the wolf getting to his sheep.'

Migration Of The Messenger Of Allah

The Quraysh and their allies made the decision that Muhammad had to be physically eliminated in order to finish with him and his religion once and for all. However, whoever did this would have to deal with the consequences and face the wrath of the respectable Bani-Hashim clan. In order to divide the guilt between as many clans and tribes as possible, forty clans were involved in the task.

The best warrior from each clan is chosen for the task. They were instructed to storm the house of Muhammad and every single one of them was to ensure to strike Muhammad with his sword at least once. This was so that if Bani-Hashim, Muhammad's clan, were to seek revenge for his blood, they would be confronted with forty clans, and thus making it impossible for them to seek any retribution.

The Almighty instructed the Prophet Muhammad to leave for the city of Yathrib, which later became known as Medinat al-Rasul or the City of the Messenger, or Medina for short. In 622 CE, after some thirteen years of calling the people to Islam, the Messenger of Allah left Mecca for Medina.

The Prophet Muhammad asked Ali son of Abu Talib to stay behind to deal with a number of issues, and Ali volunteered to sleep in the Prophet's bed acting as a decoy. The Messenger of Allah managed to slip through those who were surrounding his house just before they stormed it. When they stormed the house to kill him they found Ali instead in the Prophet's bed with no sign of their target.

On his way out of Mecca, Abu Bakr came across the Prophet as he was leaving the city, and asked the Prophet where he was going at that time. The Prophet Muhammad could not tell him other than the truth, and thereafter the Messenger of Allah asked him to join him on his migration to Medina, in order to keep the news of this mission secret until he was out of danger.

With first daylight, the forty brave warriors set off in pursuit of the Prophet by following his track. They used an expert guide to help them track him, and the guide led the warriors to the cave of Thawr, some five miles outside Mecca, where the Prophet Muhammad and his companion were actually inside, but the pursuers did not enter the cave.

It is reported that the pursuers did not enter the cave since by the time they had arrived, through divine intervention, a spider had spun its web across the opening of the cave, and a pigeon had placed its nest near there, after the two had entered the cave. The chasers did not attempt to enter the cave on the presumption that had anyone entered the cave, the spider web and the pigeon nest would have been disturbed.

Having failed to capture the Prophet, the Quraysh announced a reward of 100 camels for anyone capturing him or giving information leading to his capture.

The Prophet Muhammad left Mecca on the eve of the first day of the lunar month of Rabi-I, and arrived on the outskirts of Medina, some 400 km north of the city of Mecca, on Monday, the 12th day of the same month.

Another task that Ali ibn Abu Talib had to do when the Prophet left Mecca was to return any goods and valuables that people had given to the Prophet for safekeeping. Many of those who were the Prophet opponents also used to give their valuables to the Prophet for safekeeping every time they went on a long journey and such like. This was because the Prophet was recognized for his trustworthiness even towards his foes. They could not trust their best friends for safekeeping of their valuables, but they trusted Muhammad, Al-Amin (the trustworthy one). Ali returned all the goods and valuables that were given to the Prophet for safekeeping, including those of the Prophet's foes.

After Ali had returned all the goods the Prophet Muhammad had given him to their rightful owners, he went to the roof of the Kabah and yelled at the top of his voice, "if anyone has any claim against Muhammad, or had entrusted him with anything that he has not got back yet, then they should come forward."It has been reported that nobody did.

Having discharged all his tasks in Mecca, Ali set off for Yathrib together with his mother Fatimah bint Asad, Fatimah the daughter of the Prophet, and Fatimah daughter of Zubair.

Messenger Of Allah Arrives At Medina
When the news of the Messenger's exodus from Mecca to Medina reached the Muslims in Medina, they began to go every morning to the lava fields and wait there until the heat of noon drove them back. Many days they waited until one day when they returned to their houses, it so happened that a Jewish man was looking out from his fortress when he saw the Prophet shimmering in the haze. No sooner had he sighted him than he hailed the Muslims at the top of his voice saying:

"O Muslims, here is your Master whom you await!"

The Muslims immediately rushed to meet the Messenger of Allah on the crest of the lava fields. He then kept

going until they had reached Quba where he stopped
with the clan of Amr ibn Awf. The Muslims hailed
'Allahu Akbar' (God is Greatest) with joy at his arrival.
The Prophet stopped at Quba for three days awaiting the
arrival of Ali. He did not want to enter the Medina
without Ali.

The Prophet remained with the clan of Amr ibn Awf for
a day or two along with Ali. During his stay in Quba he
established the mosque of Quba, and thus it became the
first ever mosque established in Muslim era.

And on the Friday, the Prophet entered the Quba mosque
and led the Muslims in the Friday prayers and gave a
sermon. And this was the first Friday sermon ever given.
The Prophet prayed in the direction of Jerusalem and one
hundred men prayed behind him. After performing the
prayers, the Prophet mounted his camel. He headed
towards Medina along with Ali, who never left his side,
and the rest of Muslims.

Once in Medina, Muslim families invited the Messenger
of Allah to stay with them. In order not to turn down the
request of any one of them, the Prophet decided that he
would stay with the family by whose house his she-
camel would stop. He said: "Let her be for she is being
ordered."The camel kept on walking until she reached
the door of the house of Abu Ayyub, who happened to
be amongst the poorest in Medina.

Then Abu Ayyub hurried to the Prophet's baggage and
took it into his house. Abu Ayyub's mother, who was

blind, said: "O if only I had sight so that I could see my master the Messenger of Allah!"The Prophet Muhammad then called to Allah for her and her eyes opened. This was the first of his miracles in Medina.

It is said that when the Messenger of Allah entered Medina, it was the most joyous occasion ever witnessed by the people. One eyewitness said: "I saw the day when he entered Medina and I have never seen a brighter or better day than that day. And I saw the day he died and I have never seen a worse or darker day than the day on which he died."

First Muslim Community
With a significant number of those who embraced Islam migrating from Mecca to Medina, as well as the majority of the natives of Medina, it could be said that the first Muslim community began to take shape in the city, under the guidance of the Prophet.

Through his teachings, the Messenger of Allah brought about harmony and peace between the different rivalries and warring groups and tribes of the city and its surroundings. Whereas prior to his arrival, greed, enmity and wars prevailed between the inhabitants, in a short space of time the Prophet managed to sow the seeds of a peaceful cohesive order to the extent that they shared everything they had amongst themselves and with the Muslim migrants from Mecca despite their poverty.

With the city of Medina being some 400 km north of Mecca, some of the Muslims considered it to be a reasonably safe distance from the Quraysh who were mostly in Mecca. However, the Quraysh and their allies did not relent, and they forced the Muslims of Medina into a number of battles and skirmishes. These were usually unequal, especially at the early days, with the Quraysh and their allies being superior in number and armor. For example at the battle of Badr, which was one of the early clashes between the two sides, the Muslims combatants were 313 men, who had seventy camels and two horses, while their opponents were about one thousand, had seven hundred camels and one hundred horses.

Peace between the two sides was eventually brought about through the peace treaty of Hudaybiyah - signed in the eleventh month of the sixth year after Hijrah - which was highly biased in favor of the Quraysh and their allies, to the extent that some of the companions of the Prophet protested to him for agreeing and signing a treaty that was 'unfair and unacceptable'. However, subsequent events after the Hudaybiyah were pointedly in the interest of the Muslims, which in turn exonerated the Prophet's judgement and decision, and proved his wisdom and farsightedness.

Mecca Liberated

Less than two years after the treaty of Hudaybiyah, Quraysh grew impatient with the environment of peace and security that reigned in the land. Muslim losses in the battle of Mutah in north Arabia - in today's Jordan - encouraged the Quraysh to stir up unrest in the land and break the treaty that they had signed with the Messenger of Allah at Hudaybiyah. They began to distribute weapons to their allies and urged them to attack the allies of the Muslims at night, in breach of the peace treaty they had with the Muslims.

The Messenger of Allah left Medina on a Friday in the month of Ramadan in the eighth year of the Hijrah. He took with him all the Muslim troops which numbered ten thousand and nearly four hundred horsemen. Then the Messenger of Allah proceeded until he arrived at Marr al-Dhahran, the heights of Mecca, in the evening. He ordered his companions to light more than ten thousand fires. News of his progress had been kept hidden from the Quraysh who were concerned and feared that he might attack them.

It is reported that Abu Sufyan, the Prophet's archenemy, was saying: "I have never seen such fires as last night nor such a camp." He said: "What is the news and what are all these fires?"
The narrator responded to him: "The news is that the Messenger of Allah has arrived here. He has come with a force you cannot resist; with ten thousand of the Muslims."

Abu Sufyan said: "What is to be done?" I said: "By Allah, if he defeats you he will surely strike off your head. So ride this donkey with me so that I can take you to the Messenger of Allah and I will ask him for an amnesty for you." So he rode behind me.

It is related that Ali ibn Abu Talib said to Abu Sufyan ibn al- Harith: "Go to the Messenger of Allah and say to him what Joseph's brothers said to Joseph:

"By Allah, Allah has preferred you over us and we have certainly been sinful. (12:91).
Then the Messenger of Allah said in answer to him and seeking to behave best to him in speech: "He said:

Let there be no reproach upon you this day. Allah will forgive you and he is the Most Merciful of those who show mercy."(12:92).
The banner of the Muslims was with Saad ibn Ibadah and when he passed by Abu Sufyan he said to him: "Today is the day of slaughter, today the women will be captured."Abu Sufyan heard him and kept it to himself until the Messenger of Allah passed by him when he said: "Do you know what Saad ibn Ibadah has said?"The Messenger of Allah said: 'What he has said is of no consequence.' Then he sent someone to Saad and took the banner from him and passed it to Ali and said: "Enter with kindness."

Ali took the banner and began to proclaim: "Today is the day of mercy, today honor will be protected."Then the Messenger of Allah turned to Abu Sufyan and said to him: "O Abu Sufyan, proceed to Mecca and let them know of the sanctuary."

When the Messenger of Allah entered Mecca, a tent was pitched for him by the grave of his uncle Abu Talib. He refused to enter his house or the houses of his

companions in Mecca that had been confiscated by the
Polytheists.

Then the Messenger of Allah, after having rested a little
in his tent, bathed and mounted his camel and set out for
the sacred mosque. The Muslims were before him and
behind him and all around him and they were repeating
along with the Messenger of Allah the words of Allah
Almighty:

The truth has come and falsehood has perished, indeed
falsehood is (by nature) perishing."(17:81).
Mecca resounded with the sound of their voices until he
entered the sacred mosque and approached the black
stone at the corner of the Kabah, and kissed it. Then he
circled the House upon his camel and with a bow in his
hand. Around the House there were some three hundred
and sixty idols and he began to strike at them with his
bow saying, while the idols fell upon their faces:

The truth has come and falsehood has perished, indeed
falsehood is perishing… (17:81).
and,

The truth has come and falsehood will not revive again
and will not return. (34:4).
Then he raised Ali upon his shoulders so that he could
bring down the rest of the idols, which were upon the
Kabah. And thus a whole era of idol worshipping in
Arabia was brought to an irreversible end, and Mecca
was liberated. The conquest of the Capital City of the
idolaters and the liberation of the holy city of Mecca at

the hands of Prophet Muhammad took place without
bloodshed.

The Prophet, however, never again took his birth city,
Mecca, as his abode. The Prophet only stayed in the city
for fifteen days to manage its affairs. He appointed Etab
ibn Osayd, who was twenty-one years of age, as the
city's governor when he left the city of Mecca for
Medina.

Ideal Islamic Order

From early days, the Prophet gradually established an
Islamic system of governance and a way of life. In its
first years, the nascent Muslim community in Medina
had to contend with a number of attacks and onslaughts
by the Quraysh and their allies. The Prophet used every
opportunity to teach the Muslims the right code of
conduct for a Muslim in times of war and peace; from
personal and ethical qualities they must aspire for, to
social, political and fiscal policies.

On the political front, the Prophet enjoined the
community to avoid wars and violence as much as
possible, and it should only be the absolute last resort,
when all other avenues have been exhausted. The
Prophet Muhammad went out of his way to avoid
conflict and violence, and it is recorded that in the ten
years that the Prophet was in Medina, despite the many
battles that the Muslims were drawn into, a total of some
800 men were killed on both sides throughout the period.

The Prophet instructed his army against destroying houses or pillaging or cutting down trees bearing fruits. He ordered them not to draw out their swords except when in dire need. He used to rebuke some of his generals and physically amend for their mistakes.

Another social-political principle instilled by the Prophet Muhammad was that "Land belongs to Allah and whoever develops it". This had a very significant impact on the development of the country both socially and politically, not to mention the economic progress and revival it entailed.

Another socio-economic policy was established by the Prophet's declaration "I am responsible for them". He who died and left behind a family who would not have enough to make ends meet, then the Prophet would be responsible for them and they should go to him. On the other hand, "he who died and left a wealth behind, it was for his heirs". All the wealth was for the family the departed left behind, i.e. there was no inheritance tax in Islam.

This policy did not stop there, and it went further when the Prophet announced that if a person died and left behind a debt, then he (Muhammad, and subsequently the leader of the Islamic state in general) was responsible for repaying it .

The Prophetic legislation also addressed the interest of the non-Muslims living under the Islamic state, referred to as dhimmy; literally means "the responsibility of"(the Islamic state): "He who hurts a dhimmy, then indeed he has hurt me". Such laws, and the peaceful liberation of Mecca, encouraged many to come and live under the Islamic State, for there were guarantees of at least economic and security for them and their families, in the present and in future. People started to embrace Islam as a way of life en masse. Thus came the divine revelation:

By the name of Allah, the Compassionate, the Merciful

When came Allah's succor and the conquest, (110:1).
And thou saw the peoples entering into the religion of Allah in troops (110:2).
So glorify the praise of thy Lord and seek His forgiveness, indeed He is accepts repentance. (110:3).

The Two Momentous Things

In the holy city of Medina, Messenger of Allah ensured that he addressed the two most vital issues during his lifetime, so that these should be the sanctuary, guide and leader for the Muslims after his departure from this life. These were the compilation of the Holy Qur'an as a bound copy, and the appointment of his successors to lead the nation after him. Both of these, he did on direct instructions from the Almighty.

The Holy Quran

The Prophet ensured arrangements be made to compile a 'bound' copy of the Holy Qur'an - known at the time of the holy Prophet, and also today, as the mus-haf. The Messenger of Allah commissioned Ali son of Abu-Talib to gather and compile the entire Qur'an, which Imam Ali did during the lifetime of the holy Prophet and under his supervision.

The Messenger of Allah validated and authenticated the end result - the mus-haf - even verifying the order and position of the individual verses within a given chapter or surah, as instructed by the Almighty. According to traditions, when archangel Gabriel used to reveal a particular ayah or verse to the Prophet, the former would also indicate its position within the surah or chapter of the Qur'an and the surah that it belonged to.

Reports state that during the lifetime of the Prophet, when the entire text of the Holy Qur'an was committed to writing and it had been compiled as mus-haf, people used to come to the mosque of the Prophet, where the compiled Qur'an - mus-haf - was kept by the pulpit, to make their copies of the Holy Scripture.

It is sometimes stated, through a minor misunderstanding, that the Holy Qur'an was first compiled during the reign of the third ruler Uthman ibn Affaan, some twenty years after the death of the Prophet Muhammad. The root of this misunderstanding stems from the incorrect assumption of the meaning of the Arabic word jame that means 'to collect'. Instead it was taken to mean 'to compile'.

What was in fact commissioned at that time was to collect the incomplete documents holding some verses or chapters of the Holy Qur'an and to complete them as copies of the entire Qur'an. Any compilation that took place during this time was to reproduce the authentic copy of the Holy Qur'an as per the version compiled by Imam Ali during the lifetime of the Prophet Muhammad and under his supervision.

The Ahl Al-Bayt

The Prophet Muhammad brought about a nation and a civilization that in a relatively very short space of time won the prime position amongst all other nations. The Muslims attained such achievement so long as they adhered to the teachings of the Prophet Muhammad. Today even though the Muslims are numerous, they do not occupy the eminent station amongst the nations anymore, because they did not adhere to "the two momentous things"that the Prophet Muhammad left behind for them. The Muslim nation may still be a candidate to lead mankind to bliss and prosperity if they ensure to adhere to the teachings of the Prophet Muhammad and his successors.

Chapter 2:
Sublime Qualities Of The Prophet Muhammad.

The Prophet Muhammad, the final Messenger and Apostle of God, may Allah bless him and his family, had the greatest of morals in all aspects of life. When Imam Ali son of Abu Talib, peace be upon them, was asked about this he said: 'How can I describe the morals of the Prophet when God himself has testified that they are 'sublime' when He said:

And most surely you have sublime morals. (67:4).
The Prophet's wife, when asked about his morals answered: 'The morals of the Apostle of God were an embodiment of the Qur'an.'

Before the advent of his prophetic mission he acted under the supervision of God and was being prepared according to a divine plan to be a living embodiment of loftiness and eminence. This divine preparation was alluded to by Commander of the Faithful Imam Ali ibn Abu Talib who knew the Prophet better than anyone else among the Muslims, when he said: "From the time that he was weaned, God placed him day and night in the company of the greatest of His angels to show him the path of virtue and the most excellent morals of the world."

His Dealings With The People

It is related that Husayn, son of Imam Ali, peace be upon them both, said: "I asked my father about how the Apostle of God, may Allah bless him and his family, would spend his time indoors. He said: 'When he sought the refuge of his house he would divide his time into three parts; one part for God, one part for his family, and one part for himself. Then the part that was for him, he would divide between himself and the people; both those close to him and the general public, and he would spare all the time that he could for them.

His policy regarding the time he set aside for the Muslim community was to favor the virtuous with his manners and he divided his time according to their virtue in the religion. Among them were those who had a single need, those who had two needs, and those who had a number of needs. He would concern himself with them and occupy them with what would benefit both them and the community by asking about them and getting them to inform him of what was needed. He would say: 'Let those present inform those who are absent and whoever is not able to inform me of his needs then let someone else do it on his behalf."

Imam Husayn relates: "Then I asked my father about how the Apostle of God spent his time outside the house. He said: 'The Apostle of God, may Allah bless him and his family, would guard his tongue except in matters that concerned him. He would work to unite the people and not divide them. He would honor the nobles of every people and place them in authority over them.

He would warn the people against discords. He would be on his guard with the people at all times but would never withhold from them his smile or good manners. He would miss those of his companions who were absent and would ask the people about the affairs of the people, and would encourage what was beautiful and good and discourage what was ugly and bad.

He was balanced and did not go to extremes and would never become heedless for fear that the people would become heedless and divert from the right path. He was prepared for every situation and would not fall short of the truth nor go beyond it. It was the best of the people who followed him. In his view the best of them were those who gave the best counsel and the highest in station were those who gave the best solidarity and support."

Imam Husayn relates: "Then I asked my father about his gatherings. He said: 'Whenever the Apostle of God sat down to a meeting or stood up from one he would always be in remembrance of God, glory be to His name. Whenever he sat with some people he would always stay until the end of the gathering and would order others to do the same. He would give each of those present his due so that everyone would think that they were the most honored person present.

Whenever he sat with someone or stood with him about a matter, he would patiently wait until the other person was satisfied and left. If anyone asked him for anything he would either give him what he asked or speak to him some kind words. His openness and good manners enveloped the people and he was to them as a father; for him all of them had equal rights.

His gatherings were gatherings of kindness and modesty, patience and trust, where voices were not raised and sanctity was not trampled upon. There the people vied with each other to be the most just and the most virtuous and God-conscious. They would respect the elders and treat the young with mercy and give preference to those in need and protect the stranger."

Imam Husayn also relates that his father said: "The Apostle of God was constantly smiling, and very easy to get along with.

He was not uncouth or hard-hearted, loud voiced or immodest. He would not seek to find faults with people, or to flatter people.

He would ignore and avoid that which he did not like. However, no one would lose hope from him nor would he disappoint anyone.

He forbade himself three things: showing off, excess in anything and interfering in those things, which did not concern him.

He held back three things from the people: he would not condemn or rebuke anyone, nor would he seek out another's secrets, and would only speak in matters in which he sought a divine reward.

When he spoke his companions lowered their heads as though birds had landed upon them6 and when he fell silent they spoke. They would not vie with each other to speak, and when he spoke they would pay attention until he had finished. They spoke with him as they spoke normally; he would laugh with them when they laughed and be amazed when they were amazed. He would bear the uncouth language and questions of a stranger with patience.

He would say: 'If you see someone in need then aid him'. He would not accept praise except from his equals. He would never interrupt another person when he was speaking until he asked permission or until the speech had ended or the other person stood up to leave.

It is related that Zayd ibn Thabit said: 'When we sat with the Prophet and we began to talk about the afterlife he would join in with us. If we began to talk about worldly affairs he would also join in with us. If we began to speak about food and drink he would also join in with us.'

It is related that Imam Ali said: 'The Apostle of God, may Allah bless him and his family, whenever he saw that one of his companions was dejected he would joke with him to delight him.'

Anas said: 'Whenever the Apostle of God he passed by some children, he would always greet them.'

Asma daughter of Zayd relates: 'The Prophet, when he passed by some women, he greeted them.'Whenever any of his companions or anyone else called him he always said: 'At your service.'He would always call his companions by their kunyas to honor them and win their hearts over and would always give a kunya to those who did not have one after which that person would be known by this kunya. He would also give kunyas to the ladies who had children and those who did not. He would also give kunyas to youngsters to soften their hearts."

The Apostle of God was among the most courteous of people. He would not hold back even on cold mornings from going to a male or female servant or a child and washing their face and hands for them. Whenever someone asked him something he always paid attention and would always wait until the other person had left so that he himself would not be the first to leave. Whenever someone offered him his hand he would accept it.

Ibn Abbas relates: 'The Apostle of God, may Allah bless him and his family, would sit upon the earth, and eat upon the earth. He would milk the ewe, and respond to the invitation for food from the freeman and the slave even for the simple trotter meal.' Imam al-Sadiq peace be upon him relates: 'Whenever the Apostle of God entered a meeting place he would always sit in the lowliest place in the gathering.'

The prophet's wife was asked: 'What does the Prophet do in private?' She said: 'He sews his clothes and mends his shoes and does what a man usually does when he is with his wife.'

He used to say: 'There are five things I will not stop doing until I die; eating on the floor with the servants, riding on the saddle of a donkey, milking goats with my hand, wearing wool, and greeting children, so that these may become traditions of humility for others after I am gone.'

Imam Hasan, peace be upon him, in a tradition about the manners of the Apostle of God says: 'No, I swear by Almighty God that he would never lock himself behind doors, nor let doormen or guards keep him concealed, he would not be occupied by being served with morning or afternoon meals, . . . but rather he was in full view. Whoever wished to meet the Prophet of God could do so. He would sit upon the ground and place his food on the ground and wear rough clothes and ride upon a donkey and let others ride behind him...'

It is related that Ibn Abi Awfa said: 'The Apostle of God did not disdain or consider himself to be above walking with widows or paupers and fulfilling their needs.'Anas ibn Malik relates: 'No-one was more beloved to his companions than the Apostle of God. When they saw him they would never stand up as they knew how much he hated that.'.

'When he spoke those present would lower their heads as though birds had landed upon them and when he fell

silent they would speak and they would not vie with
each other to speak.'

Orwah ibn Masud al-Thaqafi described the depth of the
Muslims' love for the Apostle of God and their
commitment and obedience to him, when the Quraysh
sent him as a delegate for the question of the peace treaty
of al-Hodaybiyah. Orwah said addressing the Quraysh:
'O people, I swear by Almighty God that I have been in
the presence of kings, and I have been in the presence of
the Caesar of Rome and the Chosroe of Persia and the
Negus of Abyssinia, but, by God, I have never seen a
king whose companions revere him as the companions
of Muhammad revere him. When he orders them they
make haste to implement his orders. When he performs
his ablutions they almost kill each other for seeking
blessings from the water of his ablutions. When he
speaks they lower their voices and they do not stare at
him out of reverence for him.'

Anas ibn Malik relates: 'I saw the Apostle of God when
the barber was cutting his hair. His companions had
surrounded him seeking to catch his hair in their hands
as it fell.'

It is related that Imam al-Ridha', peace be upon him,
said: 'I heard my father relating from his father, from my
great grandfather from Jabir ibn Abdullah Ansari, who
said: 'The Apostle of God was in a tent of leather. I saw
Bilal of Abyssinia who had just come out with the
leftover water from the Apostle of God's ablutions. The
people rushed to him and whoever succeeded in getting

some would wipe his face with it. Whoever did not get any would take it from the hand of his companion and wipe his face with it.'

Anas ibn Malik said: 'I served the Apostle of God for some years and he never swore at me ever, nor did he ever hit me, nor did he rebuke me, nor did he frown in my face, nor did he reproach me for being tardy in carrying out his orders. If anyone of his wives reproached me he would say: 'Let him be, for if a thing is ordained it will be.'

It is related that Anas said: 'I was walking with the Apostle of God and he was wearing a rough cloak from Najran. A Bedouin Arab approached him and pulled him so violently by his cloak that I saw that the Apostle of God's shoulder had been marked by the rough cloak. Then the man said: 'O Muhammad, give me some of God's wealth that you have!' The Apostle of God turned to him and laughed and ordered a gift for him.'

During one of the battles, one of his companions said to him:

'Invoke God against the Polytheists!' The Prophet said: 'I have been sent as a mercy and guidance and have not been sent to curse people.' The Apostle of God used to say: 'My Lord has enjoined upon me seven things: he has enjoined upon me sincerity in secret and in public, and that I forgive those who have wronged me, and that I give to those who have withheld from me, and that I maintain bonds with those who cut off from me, and that

my times of silence are spent in thought, and that
whatever I see I derive a lesson from it.'

When he left the tribe of Thuqayf after having been
insulted and tormented by them one of his companions
said: 'O Apostle of God, invoke God against them.' He
said: 'O God, give guidance to the tribe of Thuqayf and
bring them to us so that they learn Islam.'

In another account it is said: 'The Prophet never struck a
woman or a servant and indeed, he never struck a single
thing with his hand except when he was fighting in the
way of Almighty God. If ever he was harmed he would
never take revenge on the person who had harmed him
except when something sacrosanct of his had been
desecrated, then he would take action.

It is related that Imam Hasan said: 'The Apostle of God
would not be angered by the mundane world or the
matters belonging to it, but if the truth was transgressed
against then nothing could withstand his anger until he
could succor it. He would not become angry for his own
affair nor would he succor it.

The Apostle of God was persevering and steadfast to the
utmost degree. For example, when Abu Talib informed
him of what the Quraysh had been plotting for him and
for the Clan of Hashim in general he said: 'O uncle, if
they were to put the sun in my right hand and the moon
in my left hand on condition that I forgo this mission, I
would not forgo it until God makes it prevail or I perish
in the process.'He would encourage the first Muslims to

stand up to opposition and to stay with the truth and would say: 'There were those before you whose flesh and nerves would be raked to the bone with steel rakes and they would not relinquish their religion, and saws would be placed upon the middle of their heads and they would be sawn in two and they would not relinquish their religion. God will fulfil this mission until one will be able to ride from Sana to Hadharalmaut fearing nothing but God and the wolf for his flocks, but you are too hasty.'

When he visited the city of al-Taif, he was treated in the worst possible manner by the people of the city, who incited the children and slaves against him and they began stoning him until wherever he put his foot there was a stone, and they split open his head and wounded his body. However he did no more than pray and supplicate to Almighty God saying: 'O God, to you I complain of my weakness and my lack of means and my insignificance in the eyes of the people, O Most Merciful One, you are the Lord of the enfeebled ones and you are my Lord. To whom will you deliver me? To an enemy from afar who is scowling at me, or an enemy whom you have given dominion over my affair? As long as your anger is not upon me then I do not care, although Your protection is what I prefer.'

His most difficult days were during the battles of Ohud and the Confederates (al-Ahzab). In the battle of Ohud the forces of polytheism routed the Muslims after they had disobeyed the orders given by the Prophet Muhammad. Only ones to remain at the heart of the

fighting were the Apostle of God, Imam Ali, and certain
sincere companions. The Prophet was severely injured;
his nose was broken and his face was split open and he
lost copious blood until false news spread that he had
died. Despite this however, he remained steadfast until
God put an end to the adversity.

In the campaign of the Confederates, the believers were
under extreme pressure which the Holy Qur'an speaks of
saying:

And when they came upon you from above you and
from below you and when your eyes trembled and your
hearts came into your mouths and you began to have
doubtful thoughts about God. There the believers were
tested and were shaken most severely (33:11).
The Muslims were in danger of being annihilated by the
army of the Confederates who had laid siege in Medina,
and the Apostle of God witnessed all this, which was of
such severity that the perseverance of great men
vanquished before it. However, the Apostle of God
remained steadfast and optimistic of victory during this
trial and rose above it with his endurance, and by this he
gave hope to the believers and raised their spirits and
gave them strength and strengthened their trust in
Almighty God. He made plans to confront the situation
with the utmost poise and determination until God gave
victory to His servant and Apostle, and defeated the
Confederates Himself.

The Apostle of God was a supreme example in
abstinence. It is related that Ibn Abbas said: 'Once, Omar

entered into the presence of the Apostle of God who was seated upon a mat of straw fibres which had left marks upon his side. Omar said: 'O Prophet of God, it would be better if you got a couch for yourself!' He said: 'What have I got to do with this mundane world? As far as myself and this world are concerned, I am like a rider who has travelled on a hot summer's day and taken shade below a tree for an hour or so and then left it and continued his journey.'

Ibn Abbas also said: 'The Apostle of God used to go without eating every other night and his family could find nothing to eat. Mostly their bread was of barley.'

It is related that once he washed his robe and was without a robe [until it dried], or he gave his clothes to a poor person and was without clothes as he did not own another robe so he covered himself with a straw mat.

In certain Qur'anic commentaries it is said that the meaning of God's words:

Taha! We sent not this Qur'an down upon you so that you might become distressed (20: 1-2).
Is that you are not required to be so harsh with yourself to the extent that you don't have more than one set of clothes to your name so that when you give your clothes to a poor person or wash your clothes, you are without clothes and have to cover yourself with straw matting.
This was an indication from God that He would be pleased with the Prophet even if he was less of a model in abstinence.

He was also a model of mercy and kindness. It is related:

'The Prophet if he heard, during prayer, a child crying he would hasten the end of prayer so that the child's mother, who was praying with the Prophet, could go to the child.

Someone said to him: 'O Apostle of God, you made the prayer lighter today!' He said: 'I heard a child crying and I feared that his mother would be concerned.'It is related that the Apostle of God smiled when some prisoners of war were brought before him. One of the prisoners said: 'O Muhammad, you take us prisoner and then you smile?' He said: 'I smiled because I want to take you towards felicity and Paradise, whereas you want to flee towards wretchedness and Hellfire.'

It is related that Maysarah ibn Mabad said: 'A man came to the Prophet and said: 'O Apostle of God, we were a people of the Ways of Ignorance, and we worshipped idols and killed our children. I had a daughter and she was always delighted when I called her. So one day I called her and she followed me and we went to a nearby well belonging to my family. There I took her hand and threw her into the well. The last thing I heard from her was her saying: 'Daddy, daddy." The Apostle of God wept until his eyes were blinded with tears.'

The Apostle of God's forgiveness and kindness was not confined to human beings but also encompassed animals. Once he saw a she camel that had been hobbling but was still loaded and it was evidently heavy for her when she was standing. He said: 'Where is her owner? Tell him that he should be prepared for a suit against him on the morrow.'42

Abd al-Rahman ibn Abdullah said: 'We were on a journey with the Apostle of God when we saw a small bird with two chicks. So we took the two chicks and the bird came flapping its wings in distress. When the Apostle of God came he said: 'Who has bereaved this bird of her children? Return her children to her.'43

He was once sitting when a pussy-cat came and slept on his sleeve. When he wanted to get up, he did not want to disturb her, so he cut off the piece of his sleeve on which she was sleeping on.

He used to say that an animal has six rights over its master: when he stops he should begin by feeding it, and if he passes by water he should offer it the chance to drink, and he should not strike it except for a good reason, and he should not make it bear more than it is able, and he should not make it walk more than it is able, and he should not sit upon it for prolonged periods while it is stationary.'

Imam Ali, said: 'Whenever the fighting became intense we would shield ourselves with the Apostle of God, may Allah bless him and his family, and no one would be closer to the enemy than him.'

Imam Ali also said: 'For the sake of the pleasure of God he went through every adversity and swallowed every bitter morsel. Those nearest to him were fickle and those furthest from him conspired against him. The Arabs prepared to make war upon him until they brought their enmity to his doorstep from the furthest outpost.' Anas said: 'The Apostle of God was the bravest of the people and the best of the people and the most generous of the people.' He said: 'One night the people of Medina were alarmed by a noise, so they set out towards it, wanting to know what was going on. The Apostle of God, who had gone before them, met them there and was saying: 'Do not fear.' He was on the horse belonging to Abu Talhah with his sword round his neck, 'Do not fear, it had just been startled.'

On the day of the battle of Ohud the Prophet suffered broken ribs and his head was laid open to the bone and his lips were wounded and blood poured onto his face. He witnessed his uncle Hamzah being killed and disembowelled. But despite all this he remained patient and concerned with Almighty God and did not panic or waver but showed great patience. It is narrated that Salim the servant of Abu Hudhayfah was wiping the blood from the Prophet's face saying: 'How can people prosper when this is the way they treat their Prophet who calls them to Almighty God.'

His Prayer
The Prophet Muhammad was passionate in his submission to God.

It is related by Husayn son of Imam Ali who spoke on the subject of the humility of the Apostle of God during his prayers saying: 'He would weep until his prayer mat became wet with tears for fear of God, but not because he had sinned for he was without sin.' On the subject of his great humility during prayer, Mutrif - son of Abdullah ibn al-Shukhayr relates of his father that he said: 'I saw the Prophet praying and his chest was humming as a boiler hums.'48 This is an indication of the reverberation in the Prophet's chest of the sound of his weeping.

In a tradition, the Prophet's wife speaks of the strength of his commitment to God saying: 'The Apostle of God used to speak with us and us with him. When the time came for the prayer though, it was as if he did not recognise us nor we him.'

Commander of the Faithful - Imam Ali, points out the importance of prayer to the Prophet and his commitment to it when he says in a tradition: 'The Apostle of God, may Allah bless him and his family, took great pains with his prayer even after he had been promised Paradise. This was due to God's words:

'And order your family to prayer and persevere in it (20:132).'
He used to order his family to prayer and made himself steadfast in it.'50

The Prophet would wait with intense longing for the time of prayer to arrive due to a tremendous yearning to stand before God in prayer. He would say to Bilal, the muezzin. who would give the call to prayer: 'Give us comfort O Bilal,'as he found his comfort in prayer and turning towards God. He persisted in worship for so long that his feet became raw, and in turning to God, and in his thankfulness for the great bounties he received from Him. When he was asked about his relentless endeavor, he said: 'Am I not to be a grateful servant?'

When Umm Salmah, the Prophet's wife, was asked about the Apostle of God's prayers at night she said: 'There is no comparison between your prayers and his. He would pray then he would sleep for the same amount of time as he had prayed. Then he would pray for the same amount of time that he had slept. Then he would sleep for the same amount of time that he had prayed. Then he would rise in the morning.'

The Prophet himself in a speech to his close companion Abu Dharr al-Ghifari55, spoke of the extent of his connection and commitment to God by way of prayer when he said: 'O Abu Dharr, God has given me happiness through prayer and has made prayer beloved to me just as food is beloved to a hungry person and water to a thirsty person. Except that if a hungry person eats he becomes full and if a thirsty person drinks he becomes satiated, but I will never have my fill of prayer.'

The Apostle of God was also greatly disposed to fasting and seclusion, to supplication and asking forgiveness from God, to praising God and making pilgrimage and giving alms. He used to say: 'One who fasts is in a state of worship even if he is upon his bed, as long as he does not slander another Muslim.' He also said: 'The sleep of

one who fasts is worship and his breathing is a
glorification of God.'

It is related that Imam Ja'far al-Sadiq said: 'The Apostle
of God used to fast until it was said of him: 'He never
breaks his fast.' Then he would eat during the day until it
was said of him: 'He never fasts.' Then he fasted on
alternate days. Then he fasted on Mondays and
Thursdays. Then he began to fast for three days of every
month: the first Thursday of the month, the Wednesday
in the middle of the month, and the last Thursday of the
month.'59

Imam Ja'far al-Sadiq also said: 'During the last ten days
of the holy month of Ramazan, the Apostle of God
would tighten his belt and seclude himself from his
wives. He would keep vigil at night and devote himself
to worship.
It is related that Anbasah, the Worshipper said: 'Up until
his death, the Prophet fasted the months of Shaban and
Ramadan and three days of every month: the first
Thursday, the middle Wednesday, and the last
Thursday.'It is related that Imam Ali said: 'The Apostle
of God fasted continuously for as long as God wished.
Then he stopped this and fasted the fast of the Prophet
David, peace be upon him: a day for God and a day for
himselff for as long as God wished. Then he stopped this
and fasted Mondays and Thursdays for as long as God
wished. Then he stopped this and fasted 'the white days':
three days every month...'

He also said: 'Almighty God has said: 'Fasting is for Me and I reward it.'

When he was seriously ill with his fatal illness, the Apostle of God came to the mosque and said: 'My Lord, mighty and majestic is He, has passed judgement and has sworn that he will not overlook the wrong of any wrongdoer. So I adjure you by God, any man of you who has been wronged by Muhammad let him stand and take his requital. For requital in this world is preferable to me than requital in the next in front of the angels and the prophets.' One man stood up who was named - 'Sawdah ibn Qays.' He said: 'May my mother and father be your sacrifice, O Apostle of God, when you came from al-Taif, I was there to greet you. You were on your camel and in your hand was your riding crop. When you wanted to set out you raised your crop and it hit my stomach and I do not know whether it was deliberate or by accident.'

The Prophet said: 'God forbid that I did it deliberately.' Then he said: 'O Bilal, go to the house of Fatimah and bring me my riding crop.' Bilal left and began calling in the alleys of Medina: 'O people, have you heard of one offering himself up for requital before the Day of Resurrection? Here is Muhammad offering himself up for requital before the Day of Resurrection!' Then Bilal brought the riding crop to the Apostle of God who said: Where is the Shaykh? (Meaning Sawdah).

The Shaykh stood up and said: 'Here I am O Apostle of God, may my father and mother be your sacrifice.'

The Prophet said: 'Come and take your requital from me to your satisfaction.' The Shaykh said: 'Then uncover your stomach O Apostle of God.' So he uncovered his stomach.

The Shaykh said: 'By my father and mother O Apostle of God, do you give me permission to put my mouth to your stomach?' The Prophet gave his permission.

The Shaykh said: 'I seek refuge in the place of requital on the stomach of the Apostle of God from Hellfire on the Day of Hellfire.' The Prophet said: 'O Sawdah ibn Qays, are you forgiving me or are you taking requital?'

Sawdah said: 'Indeed, I am forgiving O Apostle of God.' The Apostle of God said: 'O God, forgive Sawdah ibn Qays as he has forgiven your Prophet Muhammad.'[65] Asking for Forgiveness The Apostle of God would often say: 'Glory and praise be to you O God, forgive me, verily you are The Oft Forgiving, The Most Merciful.'[66]

Imam Ali Riza relates: 'The Apostle of God would not stand up from a gathering however brief without seeking forgiveness from Almighty God twenty five times.

It is related that Imam Ja'far al-Sadiq said: 'The Apostle of God used to seek forgiveness from Almighty God seventy times every day and repent to Him seventy times every day.'

Praising Almighty God

It is related that Imam Ali said: 'Whenever the Apostle of God saw something he liked he said: 'Praise be to God by whose blessings good things come to pass.'69 Imam al-Sadiq said: 'Whenever the Apostle of God found something that pleased him he would say: 'Praise be to God for this blessing.' If he found something, which disturbed him he would say: 'Praise be to God in all circumstances.'70 Imam Ja'far al-Sadiq said: 'The Apostle of God would praise God every day three hundred and sixty times,... saying: 'Great praise be to God, Lord of the worlds in all circumstances.'

The Apostle of God said: 'Give in charity even if you only give just one date, for it feeds the hungry and extinguishes your sin as water extinguishes fire.

He also said: 'When a person performs well his almsgiving, God will guarantee that the wealth he leaves behind will be well looked after.'He also said: 'Whoever wishes to prevent misfortune, then let him begin each day by giving alms.' In one of his recommendations to Imam Ali, the Apostle of God, said: 'As for almsgiving, do your utmost, until people say that you have been profligate when in fact you have not been profligate.'It is related that Jabir ibn Abdullah Ansari said: 'Never was the Apostle of God asked for something and he said no.'

In a tradition of Imam Ali's about the morals of the Prophet he says: 'He was never asked anything and said - no. He would never send away anyone who asked him something without either giving him what he asked or speaking to him some kind words.'

It is related that a man came to the Prophet and asked him for something and the Prophet gave him it. Then someone else asked him and he gave him what he wanted. Then another man came and asked him for something and the Prophet promised it to him. At this Omar ibn al-Khattab stood up and said: 'O Apostle of God, you were asked and you gave, then you were asked again and you gave, then you were asked once more and you gave your promise. You do not have to commit yourself if you do not have the means.' This speech upset the Apostle of God. Then in a show of support Abdullah ibn Hadhafah al-Sahmi stood up and said: 'Spend, O Apostle of God, and do not fear a decrease from the Owner of the Throne [i.e. God].' The Prophet was visibly pleased by this, smiled, and replied: 'This is what I have been ordered to do by God.'

The Apostle of God, would always joke with people and seek to delight them. It is related that Imam al-Kazim, peace be upon him, said: 'Often a Bedouin Arab would come and give him a gift and then he would say: 'Give me the price of my gift!' And the Apostle of God would laugh. When he was downcast he would say: 'Remember what the Bedouin did? If only he would come again.'

Once, a man came to him and said: 'Give me a mount O Apostle of God!' He said: 'I will give you the child of a she- camel.' The man said: 'And what can I do with the child of a she-camel?' He said: 'Do you know of any camels that are not born of a she-camel?'

Once he said to a woman who mentioned her husband:
'Is he the one who has white in his eye?' She said: 'He
has no white in his eye.' When she told her husband he
said: 'Do you not see that my eye is more white than it is
black?' An old woman of the Ansar said to the Prophet:
'Pray for me so that I may enter Paradise!' He said: 'But
old women do not enter Paradise!' The woman wept and
the Prophet laughed and said: 'Have you not heard the
Almighty's words describing the women of Paradise:

Indeed We created them and made them virgins, loving,
and equal in age (56): 35-37

Qualities Reflected In His Conducts

Imam Ali said in describing the Prophet: 'He was the
most open handed of people, and the most lenient of
them, and the most noble. Whoever met him and knew
him loved him...'

Imam Ali relates: 'He was the most concerned of the
people for the people, and the kindest of the people to
the people.' He also said: 'The Apostle of God whenever
he shook hands with anyone he would never withdraw
his hand until the other person withdrew his hand first.
Whenever he spoke with anyone about a need or a
matter he would never leave until the other person left
first. If anyone vied with him to speak he would always
remain silent. He was never seen pointing his feet at
anyone who sat with him. He would never send away
someone who asked him something without giving him

it or saying some kind words to him . . . when he looked
at something it would be with a glance from his eye. He
would never speak to someone in a way they disliked . . .
he would never criticise or praise food...'

The Apostle of God never criticised food. If he liked it
he would eat it and if he disliked it he would leave it.'
Imam Ja'far al-Sadiq said: 'The Apostle of God used to
divide up his glances between his companions and
would look towards one and then towards another
equally.

It is related that Abu al-Darda said: 'Whenever the
Apostle of God spoke he would smile while speaking.
Anas ibn Malik relates: 'Whenever anyone sat with the
Apostle of God and later stood up to leave, he would
also stand up to see him off out of respect.

Anas also relates: 'If the Apostle of God missed one of
his Muslim brethrens for three days, he would ask about
him. If he was absent from town, he would pray for him
and if he was present he would visit him and if he was ill
he would also visit him.'

It is also related of him that 'he did not treat anyone
harshly and would accept the apology of one who
offered it. He was always smiling except at the times
when the Qur'an descended upon him or he was giving a
sermon. He would often laugh but without guffawing . . .
if ever anyone; freeman, bondsman or woman came to
him he would always aid him or her in their needs. He
was not uncouth or hard- hearted nor one to bellow in

the marketplaces. He would never requite a bad action with a bad action but would forgive and pardon. He would offer a greeting whenever he met anyone and whoever spoke to him regarding a matter he would listen with patience until the person was satisfied and left. If he met a Muslim he would offer his hand to him...'

Once, he was in debt to a Jewish man. The man came to retrieve what he was owed but the Apostle of God said to him: 'I have nothing to give to you.' The man said: 'Then I will not leave your side, O Muhammad, until you fulfil the debt. He said: 'Then I will sit with you.'

So he sat with him until he had prayed the noon and afternoon prayers, then the sunset and evening prayers and the dawn prayer. The companions of the Apostle of God were threatening and intimidating him and when the prophet saw this he said: 'What are you doing to him?' They said: 'O Apostle of God, do you let a Jew detain you?' He said: 'My Lord did not send me to wrong a covenanter or anyone else.'

When sun arose the Jewish man said: 'I testify that there is no god but God and that Muhammad is His servant and Apostle. Divide my wealth in the way of God. I swear that I have only done what I have done so that I may see the description of you in the Torah, for I have read it there. 'Muhammad son of Abdullah, whose birthplace is Mecca and who will emigrate to Tayyibah, (Medina) he is not uncouth or hard hearted nor stern, nor does he adorn himself with indecencies or obscene language.' I testify that there is no deity but God and that you are the Apostle of God. Here is my wealth, so do with it as God orders.' This man was a very rich man too.

Once, Jurayr ibn Abdullah al-Bajali came to the Apostle of God's gathering but the place was full and he could not find a place. 'So he sat outside the house. When the Apostle of God saw him he took his robe and folded it up and threw it to him and said: 'Sit on this.' Jurayr took it and put it to his face and kissed it.

It is also related that he would accept the invitation to food of the freeman and the bondsman alike even if it were for trotter meals. He would always accept a gift even if it were a sip of milk. He would not stare in the face of anyone. He angered for the sake of his Lord and not for his own sake. He would attend funerals and visit the sick. He would sit with the poor people and eat with the paupers and give them food with his own hand. He would accept the apologies of anyone who apologised to him. He would not be superior to his servants in his food or clothing. It is related that Anas ibn Malik said: 'I served the Prophet for nine years and he never said to me 'you should have done this' and he never criticized me ever.'

Anas relates: 'I was a companion of the Apostle of God for ten years. I have smelled all types of perfume, but nothing was finer than his perfume. If one of his companions met him he would stay with him until the other man was the one to leave. If one of his companions met him and they shook hands he would not withdraw his hand until the other person did so. He never exposed his knees in front of anyone who sat with him'

It is related that Abu Said al-Khudari said: 'The Apostle of God was extremely modest and if ever he was asked for a thing he would give it. Abu Said al-Khudari also said: 'The Apostle of God was more modest than a virgin girl in her chamber. If he disliked something we could tell by his face.'

One of his characteristics was that he never frowned. If he heard someone saying something, which he disliked, he would not confront him about it but would say, "What is the matter with some people who do or say such things?"He would thus prohibit something without mentioning the name of the perpetrator.

It is related that Imam al-Sadiq said: 'The Apostle of God, may Allah bless him and his family, said: 'My Lord has ordered me to cultivate seven characteristics: to love the paupers and approach them, and to say often the words: 'there is no power or strength except through God', and to maintain the bonds of kinship even if they should cut their ties with me, and to look to those who are lower than me and not to look to those who are above me, and not to be affected in the way of God by the aspersions of the blamers, and to speak the truth however bitter it may be, and not to ask anything of anyone.'

In conclusion, some western scholars have noted that among the reasons that the people gathered round the

Apostle of God from the very first day until this day, are
his three characteristics:

• His faithfulness, for his companions at the time of his
death are those who were with him from the very first
day of his mission in Mecca.

• His simple and abstinent way of life from his early
days until death despite the fact that he became a great
ruler with wealth coming to him in abundance.

• His down-to-earth manners to the utmost degree. He
was like any one of the people and did not consider
himself superior to them.

Chapter 3:
Policies Of The Prophet At Times Of Conflict.

The Apostle of God was able to unite antagonistic, opposing and warring factions who were taken by their own egotism, nationalism, factionalism or tribalism, in a very short span of time. This was because these people recognized that the governance of the Apostle of God was consultative, compassionate, clement and merciful, and that even the most avowed of his enemies could live under its banner in complete peace and wellbeing, provided they laid down their arms. Indeed, they could live as leaders and chieftains since the Apostle had said to them: 'Testify that there is no deity but God and that I am the Apostle of God and you will be Kings.'

It was in this way that the Apostle was able to unite those warring tribes of Arabia as well as the various peoples of diverse nations. The issue was not one of color, race, nationalism, or artificial geographical boundaries and the like, but rather the issue was one of a general Islamic fraternity. Furthermore, even if a person were not a Muslim the Apostle of God would take him under his wing. For example, when the Apostle liberated the city of Mecca the majority of the people did not enter Islam but the Apostle did not coerce a single one of them to accept Islam and he granted amnesty to the wrongdoers amongst the unbelievers. What he did was to let the people sense that Islam was a better option for them than the pre-Islamic customs - better for their honor, for their property, for their persons and for their authority.

Chroniclers have mentioned that when the Apostle of God liberated Mecca he put a young man named Itab in place to govern the city and provided for him a modest stipend of four dirhams (approximately two measures of silver) daily. The Apostle of God said to him: 'Act well towards those who act well and overlook those who act wrongly.'

This was one of the reasons for the transformation of this city, from being a city of tyrants, rebels, infidels, murderers and criminals, one which had made war on the Apostle of God for twenty years, into an extremely civil city, at the hands of Itab. This was because they knew that if they acted wrongly he would overlook it and if they acted well he would act well towards them. By virtue of this constitution the city of Mecca did not rebel against the Apostle of God afterwards despite the fact that he had placed no army or security force there. Rather he had captured people's hearts with his compassion, his grace, his love and his beneficence.

When the Apostle of God came to power he said: 'Islam waives whatever came before it' 128, meaning that whoever has previously done something wrong such as spilling blood or plundering or making war or joining with the Polytheists against the Apostle will be forgiven when they enter Islam.

When the Apostle of God liberated the city of Mecca he was asked: 'O Apostle of God, will you not stay in your own house?', for the Apostle used to have a house in Mecca. He said: 'Do I have a house?' This means that the Apostle gave up his rights to the house that the Infidels had confiscated before his arrival in Mecca. He realized that the unbeliever who had taken his house was sure to have let other people stay in that house; tenants or family or the like, and that if he were to take back his house it would mean that he would have to evict those people. The Apostle did not seek to exercise even this much of his rights in case someone said: 'When the Apostle of God took control of Mecca we were living in this house and he evicted us from our dwelling and abode.'

Imam Ali did the same thing when he was pledged in as the Caliph some twenty-five years after the death of the prophet. He did not take back the land of Fadak, which was his and his sons' personal property as the inheritance of Lady Fatimah al-Zahra despite the fact that from the day he was pledged in as Caliph, it was within his power to do so.

Imam Ali was not such a worldly person that he had any need for rich furnishings and mansions and palaces and fine horses and camels and the like. He took a farsighted approach and tried to see how to unite the Muslims under the banner of Islam and how to win their hearts. Had he taken back Fadak then certainly those who had been benefiting from the lands, during the time of reign of the third ruler Othman ibn Affan, would be deprived of that benefit and would say: 'It would have been better for us had Ali not come to power.'

It is related in the traditions that an infidel who warranted death was brought before the Apostle of God. The angel Gabriel descended and said: 'O Apostle of God, your Lord conveys you a greeting of peace and says: 'Forgive this person for he is noble.' So the Prophet said to the man: 'You are forgiven so go as you please.' The man said: 'Why, O Muhammad?' The Apostle said: 'Because Gabriel has told me that you are noble and God loves the noble.' This became the reason for the man entering Islam. The Prophet had appreciated the nobility in this man and for this reason forgave him even though he was a polytheist and had committed crimes deserving death.

The Prophet Muhammad wanted to draw the people to what is best for them in this world and in the hereafter, he did not want to adhere to dictatorship or authoritarianism, or wealth and position, like other rulers, kings and Caesars do. Islam is underlined by a system of equal opportunities and respects professionalism and expertise, and therefore when it assumes power, its policy would be to forgive and forgo of acts perpetrated before, and take into account the role and impact of expertise on the society's future.

The Islamic government has certain functions:

"The preservation of social justice so that no-one transgresses against another.

"The protection of the Muslim land from enemies.

"Facilitating the nation's progress in all areas of life - order, health, employment, manufacturing and agriculture, culture and education, economics, virtue, piety, faith etc.

The ruler in Islamic lands is not to be a dictator. As Imam Ali said: 'He is not to be a ravenous lion,' meaning that he will take people's property and freedoms and stifle their breaths and limit their movements. In the Islamic regime the people's property, honor, lives, and their freedoms including those of the non-Muslims who live in the Islamic lands are guaranteed security, peace, prosperity and well-being.

It is related that the Apostle of God sent Khalid ibn al-Walid to a community of unbelievers who subsequently professed Islam but Khalid nonetheless killed a number of them. When reports of this atrocity reached him, the Apostle raised his hands to the heavens and said:

"O God, I distance myself from what Khalid has done. O God, I distance myself from what Khalid has done. O God, I distance myself from what Khalid has done. "

When Khalid came to the Apostle of God, he said: 'O Apostle of God, they only professed Islam as a ruse and a plot and falsely.' The Apostle said to him: 'Did you dissect their hearts (to see whether Islam had entered their hearts as a ruse and a plot?)'

Then Apostle of God gave Imam Ali an amount of money and said to him: 'Go to them and give them compensation for their dead.' So Ali came to them and gave them solace and gave them compensation for the animals that had been killed and gave compensation for the fear experienced by the women and for things that had been lost such as the halters of camels.

One of the chroniclers reports that when Odayy ibn Hatam saw that the Apostle of God had gained control of the area he fled from the Hijaz to Syria and was opposed to the new established government. Then one of his friends wrote to him and said: 'O Odayy, Muhammad is a Prophet and is not a king. The Prophet is merciful, kind, beneficent, consults (with others) and he is reasonable, determined and forward thinking so there is no need to flee so return to the land.'

Odayy decided to return because he trusted that friend. When he returned he stood outside the Prophet's mosque. When the Prophet emerged Odayy saw an old woman come in front of the Prophet to ask him something and the Prophet stopped for her with all kindness and answered her question and solved her problem. Odayy said to himself: 'This is not a king and this is not the behavior of sultans, kings or princes. This is the behavior of Prophets and those connected with heaven.'

It was due to this that love for the Prophet entered the heart of Odayy and he stepped forward to the Prophet and introduced himself. When the Prophet recognized him he honored him, treated him well, and greeted him with a smile and kindness and honor, and took him to his house. He entered the house of the Prophet and entered Islam at his hand when he saw the openheartedness of the Prophet and his fine morals. Then when he came out, his friend asked him: 'How did you enter Islam?' He said: 'I entered Islam because I saw the morals of the Prophets and the attributes of the Apostles in him.'

The Islamic rule of law should not only be just, but should also be beneficent. Islam has no place for torture or confiscation of wealth, and nor for executions and imprisonment, except under extraordinary circumstances; and its ruling is the same as that of the eating of carrion or the drinking of wine as is detailed in Islamic jurisprudence, which are normally expressly forbidden except when, under exceptional circumstances, not to do so would endanger one's life, such as if in a desert or such like one was dying of hunger and nothing was available but carrion. Then a person would be allowed to eat only the minimum amount to save him from death, but not to eat to be satiated.

When the people saw that Islam is merciful and that it does not execute, confiscate, torture, imprison or banish they were naturally attracted to it. The Prophet of Islam and Imam Ali adopted this policy even when they were in position to be severe and violent. Instead, they preferred to be kind and clement and forgiving even towards the criminals as can be found in many well-known accounts.

The Islamic government should also have a paradigm for granting freedoms to Islamic political parties and enhancing the progress of the people and should not interfere in the affairs of the people - not in their commerce, their agriculture, their manufacturing, their travelling, their dwelling, in expressing their opinions, in their free association, in their writings and teachings. Were the Islamic government to be a paradigm to this extent, today it would surely have attracted the eyes of the world to its excellent qualities just as the eyes of the world are still attracted to the achievements and characteristics of the Prophet Muhammad and Imam Ali.

In The Eyes Of His Opponents
It is related that Abdullah ibn Abbas said: 'A group of infidels, who had formed a pact by swearing to oppose the Prophet, met at sunset at the Kabah and said to each other:

'Send word to Muhammad and speak to him and argue with him until you leave him no excuse. So they sent someone who said to him: 'The nobles of your tribe have met so that they may address you so come to them.'

The Messenger of God came to them, while he was concerned for them; that they be guided and it was heavy upon him that they suffered by virtue of being non-believers, so he sat with them.

They said: 'O Muhammad, we have sent for you so that we may address you. By God, we do not know of a man of the Arabs who has done to his tribe what you have done. You have insulted our forefathers, criticized our religion, slandered our gods, discredited our dreams, and shattered our unity. No mean deed remains, which you have not done to us. If you have come with this speech seeking wealth then we will gather wealth for you until you are the wealthiest amongst us. If you seek rank with it then we will make you our chief. If you seek kingship then we will make you a king. If the Jinn that have possessed you have overcome you then we will pay for treatment until you are relieved of it. If you want a wife then we will marry you to the most beautiful girl of all the Arabs.'

The Messenger of God said to them: 'It is not like you say. I have not come to you with what I have come with, seeking wealth or honor or kingdom, but God has sent me to you as a Messenger and has sent down to me a book and has ordered that I be a herald of glad tidings and a warner. I have delivered the messages of my Lord and given you good counsel. If you accept what I have brought then that will be to your good fortune in this world and the next, but if you reject then I will wait for the command of God and until He judges between me and you.'

They said: 'O Muhammad, if you will not accept what we have offered, then you know that there are none whose land is less constrained than ours or with less

water or with a more difficult life, so ask your Lord who
has sent you with what he has sent you to take away
these mountains from us which confine us so that our
land may be flat and let your Lord make rivers like those
of Syria erupt in the land and let Him send your
forefathers including Qusayy ibn Kilab, who was a
master of truth, back to us so that we may ask him
whether what you say is true or false. If they confirm
you are truthful and you do as we ask then we will
believe you and by this we will recognize your station in
the sight of God and that he has sent you as a Messenger
as you say.'

The Messenger of God said: 'It is not with this that I
have been sent to you. I have only come to you from
God with what He has sent me for and I have delivered
to you that which I have been sent with. If you accept
then it will be to your good fortune in this world and the
next and if you reject then I will wait for the command
of God and until He judges between me and you.'

They said: 'If you will not do this then choose between
the following. Ask your Lord to send an angel who will
confirm what you say and will repel us from you, and if
not, then let Him make for you gardens and palaces and
treasures of gold and silver which will relieve you of
what we see you seeking; for you stand in the markets
seeking a livelihood like the rest of us. By this we can
recognize your virtue and station from your Lord if you
are a messenger as you claim.'

The Prophet said: 'It is not for me to do this, I do not ask from my Lord but He is the one who has sent me as a bringer of tidings and as a warner and if you accept then that will be to your good fortune in this world and the next, and if you reject, then I will persevere by the command of God, and until he judges between me and you.'

They said: 'Then bring the sky down upon our heads as you have claimed that your Lord can do if he wishes.'

The Prophet said: 'That is for God, if He wishes to do that with you then He will.'

They said: 'O Muhammad, then your Lord did not know that we were going to sit with you and ask you what we have asked you so that He might teach you what you should do to divert us, or inform you what He would be doing to us if we do not accept what you have been sent to us with. We have heard that a man in al-Yamamah named 'al-Rahman' teaches this to you. By God, we will never believe in this 'al-Rahman' ever. We have warned you O Muhammad, by God, we will not let you be for what you have done to us until we destroy you or you destroy us.'

Then the Messenger of God rose and left them to return to his family, with sorrow and sadness for them. Then Nadr ibn Harith ibn Kaldah got up and said, "O Quraysh! By God, you are gripped with an issue that you have not found a solution for. While Muhammad was a young man he was the most pleasant amongst you, the

most truthful in speech, and the most trustworthy of all
amongst you . . . he was so until you started to see the
grey hair in his beard, and then he came with what he
has come to you with. You said he is a sorcerer, but by
God, he is not so, for we have seen the sorcerers and we
know their traits and tricks. Then you said he is a poet,
whereas we have heard the poems and their various
categories. Then you said he is crazy, but by God, he is
not mad for we have seen madness . . . O Quraysh! Look
into this affair of yours, for by God a matter of great
importance has descended upon you.

Conducts And Strategies Of Battle

The Prophet used to consult his companions in battle and
meeting the enemy and the choice of positions. One of
the companions related: 'I have not seen anyone who
consults his companions more than the Messenger of
God.' He used to stay in the rear guard when marching to
urge on the weak ones and to seat behind him those who
became detached from the main force. He was most
attentive to his companions during marching.

If he wished to make an excursion he would keep it a
secret and make a diversion so that the killing would be
kept to a minimum. He would send out reconnaissance
and advance parties and post sentries.

Whenever he faced the enemy he would stop to pray to
God and ask for His succor. He and his companions
would invoke the name of God much and lower their
voices.

When the blows intensified the others would take him as a shield. As mentioned in Nahj al-Balaghah, Imam Ali says: 'In the heat of the battle we would shield ourselves with the Messenger of God for no-one was closer to the enemy then he was.'

He was always the closest to the enemy among his men. The Commander of the Faithful Imam Ali is quoted as having said: 'The Apostle of God forbade the use of poison against the Polytheists.'

The Messenger of God and his companions passed near by the lands of Ashja and the Damrah tribe on the way to a sortie. There was already a state of truce between Damrah and him.

The companions said to the Messenger of God: 'O Messenger of God, the Damrah are near to us and we fear that they will cross us on the way to Medina or assist the Quraysh against us, so should we attack them.'

The Messenger of God said: 'Not at all, they are the most respectful of the Arabs to their parents and the best in maintaining the bonds of kinship and most honest in fulfilling their promises.'

If he sent out a troop he would enjoin upon them fear of God and say: 'Go in the name of God and fight those who deny God. Do not mutilate and do not betray and do not kill children, women, and old men.'

He would also say: 'Go in the name of God and in the way of God and upon the religion of the Apostle of God. Do not plunder and do not mutilate and do not be treacherous and do not kill old men or children or women. Do not cut down trees except when forced to do so. And if any man of the Muslims, be he of low or high rank, give respite to any of the Polytheists then he has sanctuary so that he may hear the word of God. If he then follows you then he is your brother in faith and if he refuses then send him away in safety, and seek the aid of God.'During battle he would give his men special code words and signals so that they would be known when they spoke.

He used to order the commanders of his troops to invite the enemy to Islam and migration4, or Islam only so that they would be like the Bedouins who did not have a share in the spoils of war, or to ask them to pay the Jizyah tax. If they agreed this would be accepted from them. If not, then he should seek help from God and fight them.

If he won on the day he would send out a herald and gather all the booty. He would begin with the things that had been pillaged and would return them to their rightful owners. Then he would take out a fifth (khums) of what was left and would use it for the benefit of the Muslims as instructed by the Almighty. Then he would use some of the rest for those who did not have a normal share like the women and the children and the servants. Then he would distribute the remaining bulk equally amongst the army: a horseman would get three shares, one for himself and two for his horse and the foot soldier would get one share. He would treat the strong and the weak alike in the share of the spoils except in the share of public estates.

With The Prisoners Of Battle Of Badr
When the prisoners of the battle of Badr5 were brought forth, the Messenger of God divided them amongst his companions and said: 'Treat the prisoners well.'

Abu Aziz ibn Omeir ibn Hashim the brother of Masab ibn Omeir was amongst the prisoners. He had been carrying one of the banners of the Quraysh. After he was freed he said: 'I was a captive in the hands of some of the Ansar6, when they brought me from Badr. When they prepared their food they used to favour me with the bread and they would eat dates. Bread was scarce whereas dates were the staple. This was because of what the Messenger of God had instructed about our treatment. If one of the Ansar came across even a crust of bread he would pass it to me but I would feel ashamed and return it to him. Then he would return it to me and would not touch it. Also they had very few camels and they would seat me upon a camel and they themselves would walk beside it.

When the night descended upon them and some of the companions were given the task of securing the bonds of the prisoners, the bonds of al-Abbas were made tight. The Prophet heard him complaining and because of this he could not sleep. When the Ansar heard about this they set al-Abbas free for they understood that the Prophet

would be satisfied other than with this and they asked
him to let them waive his ransom.

The Messenger of God took seventy prisoners on the day
of Badr and ransomed them according to their wealth.
Generally the people of Mecca were literate and the
people of Medina were not. Whoever did not have any
ransom money, would be sent ten youths from Medina
so that he could teach them to read and write instead.

The Messenger of God set free al-Muttalib ibn Hantab
and Saifi ibn Abi Rafaah and Abu Izzah al-Jamahi. He
only took their oaths that they would not aid anyone
against him. Abu Izzah was a needy person who had
daughters. He said: 'O Messenger of God, you know that
I do not possess any wealth and that I am in need and I
have children so set me free.' The Messenger of God did
so after taking his oath not to aid anyone against him.

Ransom Of His Son-In-Law

The Messenger of God also freed Abu al-As ibn al-
Rabiah, the husband of his (step) daughter Zainab after
she had sent ransom for him. The ransom that she sent
included a necklace, which had been given to her by her
mother Khadijah on the night of her wedding. When the
Messenger of God saw the necklace he remembered his
faithful wife Khadijah and was moved to tears. Then he
turned to the Muslims and said: 'If you see fit, let
Zainab's husband go free and send back the ransom that
she has sent for doing so.'

By this he did not impose his opinion upon them despite the Qur'an having said:

The Prophet has more authority over the believers than they do over their own selves (33:6).
In doing so he expressed the freedom available within Islam and set out its wise policies. The Muslims said: 'Yes O Messenger of God, may we and our wealth be sacrificed for you.' So they returned what Zainab had sent and set free Abu al-As without ransom and the Messenger of God thanked them for this.

The Messenger of God had obliged Abu al-As and he promised the Prophet to give Zainab freedom of movement; so when Abu al-As went to Mecca, the Messenger of God sent Zaid ibn Harithah and another man of the Ansar and said to them: 'Wait at the bottom of Yajaj until Zainab passes by then accompany her here to me.' So they set out towards Mecca and this was one month after the battle of Badr.

When Abu al-As reached Mecca he ordered her to join her father so she prepared herself and left for Medina. On the way she was attacked by Habbar ibn al-Aswad who attacked her with his spear while she was in the howdah. She was with child and as a result she miscarried and later died of the injuries she had sustained. The Messenger of God ordered that he be killed but they were not able to seize him. On the day of the liberation of Mecca, Habbar fled to the hills then returned in disguise. When he stood before the

Messenger of God he entered Islam and the Messenger of God accepted his Islam and forgave him.

Prohibition Of Torture And Mutilation
Mukraz ibn Hafs arrived to pay the ransom of Suheil ibn Amr who had been taken prisoner by Malik ibn al-Dakhsham. He was ransomed for four thousand Dirhams.

Ibn Ishaq mentions one of the companions as saying: 'O Messenger of God, let me tear out the incisors of Suheil ibn Amr so that his tongue will loll out and he will not be able to make speeches against you anywhere ever again.' The Prophet said: 'I will not have him mutilated, for God would then mutilate me even though I am a Prophet.'

In another account it is said that the Messenger of God said: 'He just might act in a way for which we would not blame him.'

Returns Evil With Good
Two sons of Abu Sufyan took part in the battle of Badr - Handhalah and Amr. Handhalah was killed and the Messenger of God took Amr as prisoner.

Abu Sufyan was offered the opportunity to pay ransom for his son Amr. He said: Am I to pay out of my money as well as out of my blood? They have killed Handhalah and now I am to pay ransom for Amr. Let him remain with you. You can hold him for as long as you want.' Meanwhile, Saad ibn al-Numan the brother of the Bani

Amr ibn Awf left Medina to make a supererogatory pilgrimage (umrah) to the holy Kabah in Mecca. Abu Sufyan attacked him and held him prisoner in lieu of his son Amr. This was despite the fact that the Quraysh had made a promise not to stand in the way of anyone who came to Mecca as a pilgrim.

The tribe of Amr ibn Awf went to the Messenger of God and informed him of their news and asked him to hand over Amr ibn Abu Sufyan so that they could secure the release of their brother. The Messenger of God agreed and he was sent to Abu Sufyan who in turn set free Saad.

Gives His Foes The Choice Of Peace
When the Messenger of God first entered Medina he made a peace treaty with the Bani Nadeer tribe as he did with the rest of the Jewish tribes with condition that they would not fight him nor he would fight with them and he accepted these terms. When the Messenger of God fought at Badr and defeated the Polytheists they said: 'By God, he certainly is the Prophet whom we find described in the Torah.'

When he fought at hud and the Muslims were defeated they were seized with doubts and they broke their treaty. They went to the Quraysh and formed an alliance and a pact with them that they would stand united against Muhammad.

Then Gabriel descended and informed the Prophet of this. In order to expose the antagonistic intentions that the Bani Nadeer held against the Muslims, he went out to them on a Saturday during the month of Rabi-I and prayed in the mosque of Quba along with Imam Ali and few of his companions. Then he approached them and spoke to them of a loan to pay some reparations (there was a loan agreement in force between them) and they agreed to make the loan.

Then some of them spoke in secret to others saying: 'Never again will you find him in such a situation.' He was beside a wall of one of their houses. They said: 'Who will climb onto this house and throw this rock on him and kill him and relieve us of him?' Amr ibn Jahhash volunteered saying: 'I will do it.' Salam ibn Mushkam said: 'Do not do it, God will surely inform him of what you intend. It is a breach of the treaty that is between us and him.'

Then Gabriel came and informed the Messenger of God of the news and thus he returned to Medina. Then his companions caught up with him and said: 'You left O Messenger of God, and we did not realize it.'

He said: 'The Jews sought to betray me and God informed me of this so I left.' Then he sent a messenger to the Jews ordering them to leave their homes. Their houses were in a nearby village called Zahrah, towards al-Far district. He gave them ten days to leave.

The news reached Ibn Obayy and he sent a messenger to the Jews telling them not to leave their homes and promising them the assistance of his people and reinforcements from the Jewish clan of Bani Qureidhah

and their allies the clan of Bani Ghatfan. They sought
this.

So the Messenger of God went out to them and prayed
the afternoon prayer in the courtyard of the Bani Nadeer
tribe. Imam Ali carried the banner and Ibn Umm
Maktum was left in charge of Medina. When they saw
the Messenger of God, they took refuge in their
fortresses with arrows and stones. Then the clan of
Qureidah left them, and Ibn Obayy betrayed them. Then
the Messenger of God laid siege to them for twenty-one
nights.

God put terror into their hearts and they eventually
decided to leave Medina without fighting. The
Messenger of God said to them: 'Leave the city and you
will save your blood and whatever your camels can carry
except for weapons.' So they left with their women and
their children playing the pipes and banging tambourines
having laden six hundred camels with their property.
People even tore out the doors of their houses and loaded
them onto camels. Then they destroyed their houses with
their own hands and left. Some of them went to Khaybar
and others went to Syria and some went to al-Hirah.

His Magnanimity
During one excursion, the Messenger of God rested
under a tree by the side of a river. Then the river flooded
and came between him and his companions. He was seen
by one of the Polytheists who said to his companions: 'I
will kill Muhammad.' So he approached and threatened
the Messenger of God with his sword and said: 'Who

will save you from me?' The Messenger of God said:
'My Lord and yours.'

Then Gabriel blew him from his horse and he fell. The
Messenger of God stood up, took the sword and sat on
the man's chest and said: 'Who will save you from me?'

The man said: 'Your goodness and generosity.' So the
Messenger of God left him. The man stood up and went
to his people and said: 'I have just come from the best of
people.' Many people entered Islam because of him. In
another account it is said that when he sat on his chest he
said to him: 'Will you testify that there is no deity but
God and that I am His messenger?' the man said: 'I
promise that I will not fight you nor will I be with any
people who fight you.' So he let him be on his way. Then
the man came to his people and said: 'I have just come
from the best of people...'

His Care For His Companions
The Messenger of God used to travel in the rear guard so
that he could help the weaker of his companions and
carry those whose mounts had faltered and were no
longer able to bear a burden. On the way back from the
Patched Banner excursion he met with Jabir ibn
Abdullah al-Ansari who had lagged behind the rest and
he said to him: 'What is wrong O Jabir?'

Jabir, pointing to his camel said: 'This has made me
slow.' The Messenger of God approached the camel and
ran his hand over it and it became strong and began
making advances to the Messenger of God's she camel.

Then he said to Jabir: 'O Jabir, will you sell me this
camel of yours.' He said: 'Rather I will gift it to you.'

He said: 'No but sell it to me.' So the Messenger of God
offered an ounce of gold when he said: 'Are you satisfied
O Jabir.' Jabir said: 'I am satisfied O Messenger of God,
the camel is yours.' The Messenger of God said: 'It is
mine and you may ride it until we reach Medina.' Then
he said to Jabir: 'Are you married O Jabir?' He said: 'Yes
O Messenger of God.'

He said: 'Was she a divorcee or a virgin.' He said: 'A
divorcee.' Then Jabir sighed deeply and said: 'O
Messenger of God, on the day of (the battle of) Ohud my
father was (fatally) wounded and I was left in charge of
seven of my sisters so I married a woman who could
take care of them.'

The Messenger of God was concerned and it showed in
his face and he said praising what Jabir had done: 'You
have done well O Jabir.'

Then the Messenger of God asked about his father's
debts and Jabir informed him. Then the Messenger of
God said to him: 'When you enter Medina and want to
clip your date palms and take the dates then let me
know.'

Jabir relates: 'So I entered Medina and told my wife of
what had been said to me by the Messenger of God and
she said with joy: 'You must obey.' In the morning Jabir
took the camel to the door of the mosque then sat

nearby. The Messenger of God came to the mosque and saw the camel and said: 'What is this?' 'O Messenger of God, this is Jabir's camel.' said some of his companions.

He said: 'And where is Jabir himself?' So Jabir was called upon and the Prophet said to him: 'Take the camel for it is yours.' Then he summoned Bilal and said to him: 'Give Jabir an ounce of gold.'

Jabir relates: So I went with him and he gave me an ounce.

He Goes Hungry

The Messenger of God used to bind stones upon his stomach because of hunger.

Imam Ali relates: 'We were with the Prophet digging the moat before the battle of the Khandaq when Lady Fatimah came with a crust of bread. She gave it to the Prophet who said: 'O Fatimah, what is this?'

Lady Fatimah said: 'I baked a loaf of bread for Hasan and Husayn and I have brought you this crust. The Prophet said:

'This is the first food to enter your father's stomach for three days.'

Foe Turned Into Friend

The Messenger of God sent some horsemen to Najd led by Muhammad ibn Musallamah. They captured a man of the Banu Hanifah named Thamamah ibn Othal who had previously killed some Muslims. They brought him to

Medina and tied him to a pillar in the mosque. (In
another account it is said that they left him in a room
adjoining the mosque.)

The Messenger of God went to see him and said to him:

'What is your situation O Thamamah?' He said: 'It is
good O Muhammad. If you kill me you will kill a person
of noble blood. If you let me go you will find me
grateful. Or, if you want money then ask whatever you
want.'

The Messenger of God said to his companions
afterwards: 'Set Thamamah free.'

So Thamamah went to an oasis near the mosque and
washed himself then he entered the mosque and said: 'I
testify that there is no deity but God and that
Muhammad is His Messenger. O Muhammad, I swear to
God, no face on earth was more detestable to me than
yours but now it has become the most beloved of faces
to me. No way was more detestable to me than your way
and now your way has become the most beloved of ways
to me. No land was more detestable to me than your land
but now your land has become the most beloved of lands
to me. Your horses took me when I was going to Mecca
for pilgrimage so what do you think?' The Messenger of
God gave him glad tidings and ordered him to go to the
pilgrimage. When he arrived in Mecca someone said to
him: 'Have you become rejuvenated?'

He said: 'No but I have entered Islam with Muhammad
the Messenger of God and from now on not a grain of
wheat will come to you from al-Yamamah unless the
Prophet gives permission.'

Al-Yamamah was an agricultural area that was depended
upon by the Meccans. Thamamah left for his lands and
prevented cargo from reaching Mecca until the Quraysh
suffered. They wrote to the Messenger of God calling
upon their bonds of kinship with him so that he would
write to Thamamah to let them carry food to Mecca.
Messenger of God did this.

Tolerated The Enemy Of The State
While the Messenger of God was returning from his
campaign against Bani Mustaliq tribe, a dispute had
occurred between Jahjah ibn Masud al-Ghifari of the
Muhajirun and Sannan ibn Wabr al-Jahani of the Ansar.
Abdullah ibn Obayy, who was a hypocrite from the
Ansar said: 'When we return to Medina the mighty will
surely drive out the weak.' By the 'mighty' he meant
himself and by the weak he meant 'the Prophet
Muhammad'. By declaring this slogan Abdullah ibn
Obayy tried to use the dispute to bring about a
commotion in the Muslim community and break its
unity.

As a result of the said slogan, the Ghifari called upon the
Muhajirun and the Jahani called upon the Ansar (to fight
one another with the help of their respective factions -
this would have meant the first inter-Muslim clash). The
Messenger of God said: 'Is it to be the call of the

Jahiliyyah (the Times of Ignorance) while I am still among you?' Zaid ibn Arqam told the Messenger of God of what Abdullah ibn Obayy had said and the chapter of the Qur'an named 'The Hypocrites' was revealed in this regard.

Abdullah, the son of Abdullah ibn Obayy disassociated himself from his father and came to the Messenger of God and said: 'O Messenger of God, you are the mightiest and he is the meanest. I swear that if you wish we will drive him out O Messenger of God.' He waited for his father near to Medina and said: 'Do not enter the city until the Messenger of God grants you permission to enter.'

The father complained of his son to the Messenger of God who sent word for him to let him enter. He said: 'Now the permission has come so you may enter.' He also said: 'I have heard O Messenger of God that you wish to kill my father and I fear that if you order someone other than me to do so that I will not be able to let the killer of my father walk in the land without killing him and by this entering the hellfire because of killing a believer for an infidel. The Ansar know that I am the most dutiful of them to his father. But, O Messenger of God if you intend to kill him then order me to do so and I will bring you his head.'

The Messenger of God said words of kindness to him and told him to accompany his father in a fine manner as long as he was amongst the Muslims.

His Adherence To The Peace Treaty Of Hodaybiyah
Amongst several others, one of the conditions of the
treaty of Hodaybiyah was that if anyone left Quraysh
and migrated from Mecca to Medina to join the Prophet
Muhammad and his Muslim followers without the
permission of his guardian, then he would have to be
returned to the Quraysh. However, if one of the
followers of the Prophet wanted to go back to the
Quraysh in Mecca he should be allowed to do so. The
Prophet had in principle accepted this condition, as well
as other conditions of the treaty and was ready to sign
the peace deal.

However some of the companions objected to this and
said:

'Glory be to God, how can we send a man back to the
Polytheists when he has come to us as a Muslim.' At this
stage, suddenly, Abu Jandal ibn Suheil ibn Amr entered
the gathering shackled. He had escaped from his father's
prison in lower Mecca and put himself in the hands of
the Muslims. He had committed no crime other than
choosing Islam over Polytheism.

His father Suheil said: 'O Muhammad, this is the first
person I demand that you return to me.' The Prophet
said: 'We have not finished the document yet.' He said:
'Then I will never make peace with you ever.'

The Prophet said: 'Let him remain under our protection.'
He said: 'I will not.'

The Prophet said: 'No, let it be so.' He said: 'I will not.'

In order to save the deal, Mukraz, a member of the Quraysh delegation that had come to negotiate and sign the pact, said:

'Yes, we give him over to your protection.' But Suheil refused this completely and made the whole peace treaty depend upon his son being delivered to him.

When Abu Jandal saw that he was to be returned to his father he said: 'O Muslims, am I to be returned to the Polytheists after I have come to you as a Muslim. Do you not see how I have been treated?' He had been tortured severely because of his belief in God. Some of the Muslims said: 'We will not return him.'

The Apostle of God stood up and took him by the hand and said: 'O God, you know that Abu Jandal is sincere, so relieve him and grant him a way out.' Then he approached the people and said: 'He is safe, and he will return to his father and mother. I wish to fulfil the conditions of the Quraysh.' Then he turned to Abu Jandal and said: 'O Abu Jandal, have patience and think of the afterlife. God will surely grant you and the rest of the Muslims with you relief and a way out. We have made a peace treaty with the Quraysh and given them our word and they have given us theirs. We will not act treacherously with them.'

Among The Blessings Of The Treaty Of Hodaybiyah

When the Apostle of God returned to Medina, Abu Basir ibn Oseid ibn Harithah al-Thaqafi, who was a new convert, escaped from the Polytheists of the Quraysh. They sent two men in pursuit of him who came to the Apostle of God and reminded him of the treaty. So he sent Abu Basir up to the two men.

They left and reached as far as Dhu al-Hulayfah where they stopped to eat some dates they had with them. Abu Basir said to one of the men: 'I see that your sword is a good one.' The man said: 'It is indeed, by God. I have tried it out more than once.'

Abu Basir said: 'Let me look at it.'

Then he overpowered him and struck him until he died and the other man fled to Medina and entered the mosque. When the Apostle of God saw him he said: 'This man is terrified.' The man said: 'Abu Basir has killed my companion and I was nearly killed.'

Then Abu Basir came and said: 'O Prophet of God, God has fulfilled your covenant. You returned me to them and God delivered me from them.' The Prophet said: 'He starts a war whenever there is anyone with him.' When Abu Basir heard this he knew that the Apostle of God would return him to them again. So he left with five men who had come with him as Muslims, and ended up between al-Ays and Dhil-Murrah regions in the lands of Juheinah on the road that the caravans of the Quraysh took.

Abu Jandal ibn Soheil and seventy riders who had entered Islam also escaped from Quraysh and they joined up with Abu Basir as did every Muslim that left the Quraysh until their numbers reached three hundred fighters all of them Muslims. Every time they heard of a caravan of the Quraysh leaving for Syria they would intercept it and take their property.

The Quraysh sent Abu Sufyan to the Apostle of God begging him to send word to Abu Basir al-Thaqafi and Abu Jandal and their men for them to come to him. Relinquishing one of the most important articles of the treaty of Hodaybiyah, which was designed to prevent and discourage Muslim converts to join the Prophet Muhammad, on behalf of the Quraysh Abu Sufyan said to the Apostle of God: 'Whoever leaves us for you then hold onto him without blame upon you.'

Then those who had advised the Apostle of God not to return Abu Jandal to his father realised that obedience to the Apostle of God was better for them under all circumstances. They realized that this was the greatest victory so far for Islam. Previously there were clashes and a sense of animosity between the Muslims and the infidels, but now that there was a truce and the war was over and the people were secure, whenever they met they would discuss their ideas and beliefs and whenever anyone spoke of Islam and others reasoned and understood Islam they would embrace it as a way of life. During the next two years more people entered Islam than had already become Muslims in the previous years.

Kindness To Captives

When Imam Ali conquered the Jewish fortress of
Khaybar, among the captives he took was Safiyyah the
daughter of Huyyay ibn Akhtab. He summoned Bilal
and put her in his custody and said to him: 'O Bilal, only
give her over to the Apostle of God until he does as he
sees fit with her. Bilal took her and on the way to the
Apostle of God they passed by the dead and Safiyyah
almost died of grief. When the Apostle of God heard of
this he said to Bilal: 'Have you been stripped of mercy O
Bilal?'

Then he offered her Islam and she accepted and he freed
her, and he offered to marry her, which she accepted.
She was a well-mannered woman and whenever she
wanted to mount a camel and the Apostle of God bent to
help her mount she would refuse. He saw a green mark
near to her eye and asked her about it. She said: 'O
Apostle of God, before you came to us I saw in a dream
the moon and it was as if it had left its place and
descended into my lap. I told my husband this and he
struck my face and my eye became green. He said: 'This
means nothing other than that you desire the 'King of the
Hijaz' i.e. the Prophet.

The Protectorate

When Imam Ali had conquered the important fortresses
of Khaibar and killed Marhab and his brother Yasir and
up to one hundred other Jewish braves while they had
only killed fifteen of the Muslims, the Jews were
frightened and sought refuge by way of secret tunnels in

the last castle that remained in their hands wherein was
their wealth and their foodstuffs.

The Apostle laid siege to the castle and one of the Jews
went to him and said: 'O Muhammad, will you grant me
the security of myself, my family and my possessions
and sons if I show you how to conquer the castle?'

The Apostle of God said: 'Yes you are safe.'

He said: 'You should order that this place be dug for it is
where the water of the castle runs. Then you must block
the channel and the castle will be without water and they
will surrender.' The Apostle of God refused his
suggestion and said: 'God will bring about another way.'

When the siege tightened on the Jews and they realized
that they would not be able to resist or fight, their leader
Ibn Abil-Haqiq sent word to the Apostle of God that
they wished to negotiate and asked whether he could
descend and speak with him.

The Apostle of God agreed and Ibn Abil-Haqiq
descended and made a treaty with the Apostle of God on
condition that none in the fortress would be harmed and
that the fighters would leave Khaybar, with their woman
and children and they would leave the land, animals,
wealth and weapons to the Apostle of God.

The Jews Enter Islam
When the people of Khaybar descended from their forts
under the peace treaty and prepared to leave the land,

they came to the Apostle of God with a proposal and said: 'O Muhammad, let us remain in this land and you will have one half of the crop for we know the land best and have lived here longest.'

The Apostle of God agreed on the condition that if he wished to expel them he could and if he wished that they remained, they would remain. When the crops matured, he sent Abdullah ibn Rawahah to collect the half share from them. When he came he gave them an evaluation for the crop and said: 'Either you take the crop and give us half the price or we take the crop and give you half the price.'

The Jews said: 'This is justice; by this the heavens and the earth were established.' After this they entered Islam because of what they had seen of the justice of Islam and the ethics of the Apostle of God.

It is said that when the wealth of Khaybar was divided up the Muslims were satiated and they found a comfort hitherto unknown. One of them said: 'We never ate our fill until we conquered Khaybar. Another said: 'When Khaybar was conquered we said: 'Now we will eat our fill of dates.'

Forgiveness Not Revenge
When a state of calm reigned and the Apostle of God had finished with Khaybar, the Jewess Zainab - daughter of al-Harith ibn Salam ibn Mushkam, the niece of Marhab gifted the Apostle of God a roast sheep. She had asked: 'Which part of the sheep is most liked by the

Apostle of God. They said to her: 'The shoulder.' So she put a great deal of poison there and also poisoned the rest of the sheep.

Then she brought the sheep to him and placed it before him. The Prophet took the shoulder and took a bite from it and then spat it out. Bishr ibn Barra ibn Mamur was with him and he also took a bite and swallowed it.

The Apostle of God said: 'Lift your hands, for the shoulder of this sheep is telling me that it has been poisoned.' Then the Jewess was summoned and she confessed. The Apostle of God said to her: 'What made you do this?'

She said seeking an excuse for what she had done: 'You did something to my people that I could not forgive. So I thought: 'If he is a Prophet he will be informed, and if he is a king then we will have been relieved of him.' The Apostle of God overlooked her transgression. Then when she saw the conducts and morals of the Apostle of God she entered Islam and said: 'Now I know that you are a Prophet of God and I bear witness to you and who is with you that I will follow your religion. I bear witness that there is no deity but God and that you, Muhammad, are the Apostle of God.'

A Jew's Word Was Enough
The Apostle of God remained in Medina after his return from Khaybar until the month of Shawwal in the seventh year of the Hijrah. During this time he sent some sorties to consolidate the security of Medina and to warn those

who still considered attacking the Muslims and also to deliver the message of Islam and explain its high-minded rules and teachings to them.

One such sortie was that of Osamah ibn Zaid. The Apostle of God sent him with some horsemen to a Jewish village, which was named al-Harqah, to invite them to Islam. A Jewish man named Mardas ibn Nuheik approached the horsemen saying: 'Peace be upon you. I testify that there is no deity but God and that Muhammad is the Apostle of God.' But when Osamah ibn Zaid passed by him he speared Mardas and killed him.

When Osamah returned to the Apostle of God and told him of this the Prophet said: 'You killed a man who testified that there is no deity but God and that I am the Apostle of God?'
Osamah said: 'O Apostle of God, he only said that to save himself from death.' The Apostle of God said: 'You did not lift the cover from his heart! You neither accepted what his tongue was saying nor did you know what was in his mind!'

In this regard God revealed:

And do not say to those who offer you a greeting of peace: you are not a believer (4:94).
Then the Apostle of God sent compensation to the family of Mardas ibn Nuheik.

The Bearer Of The White Banner

The Apostle of God had sent al-Harith ibn Omeir al-Azdi with a letter to the king of Busra the absolute ruler of greater Syria in which he invited him to Islam. When he stopped at Mutah the king's agent Sharhabil ibn Amr al-Ghasani arrested him and when he knew that he was the Prophet's messenger to the king he went against the prevailing customs of the time and killed him. No other messenger of the Apostle of God was killed despite the vast number he sent from Medina to kings and leaders after the treaty of Hodaybiyah.

When the news of the death of al-Harith reached the Apostle of God he was very saddened, and gathered the Muslims and told them that al-Harith had been killed as well as the group of missionaries. They made haste and left Medina and made camp at al-Jarf. The Apostle of God led them in the noon prayer, and then gave a sermon and advised them saying: 'I enjoin upon you the fear of God. Fight in the name of God and in the way of God. Fight those who disbelieve in God, and do not use treacherous means and do not plunder. Do not kill children or women or old people, and do not cut down any date palms or trees and do not destroy any buildings.'

Then the Apostle of God raised a white banner and handed it to Ja'far ibn Abi Talib whom he appointed as the commander of the squadron, and said: 'When you meet your enemy, the Polytheists then invite them to one of three things and whichever of them they choose then accept it from them and stay your hands from them: Invite them to Islam and if they agree then accept it from

them and leave them be. Then invite them to leave their
abode for the abode of the Muhajirun. If they accept,
then inform them that they have the rights and
responsibilities of the Muhajirun (the emigrants)11. If
they enter into Islam and prefer to remain in their abode
then they will be treated as the Bedouin Muslims; God's
rule will be in force amongst them but they will have no
rights over the spoils or booty until they fight alongside
the Muslims. If they refuse (these two options) then call
them to pay the Jizyah tax12and if they do so then
accept it from them and stay your hands from them. If
they refuse all this then seek the aid of God and fight
them. '

The Prophet Forgives The Traitor
The Apostle of God told the Muslim community that he
was going to Mecca and ordered them to prepare for the
journey. He said: 'O God, keep the spies and news from
the Quraysh so that we can surprise them in their lands.'
Hatib ibn Baltaah wrote a letter to the people of Mecca
informing them that the Apostle of God was coming to
them and gave the letter to a woman whose name was
Sarah, giving ten Dinars for her to take the letter to the
people of Mecca.

Sarah was the servant of Abu Amr ibn Sayfi ibn Hisham.
She had come to the Apostle of God from Mecca to
Medina. The Apostle of God had said to her: 'Have you
come as a Muslim?' She said: 'No.'

He said: 'Have you come as an imigrant?' She said: 'No.'

He said: 'What have you come for?'

She said: 'You have been my family and patrons. But my patrons have gone and I am in dire need. So I have come to you so that you may give to me and clothe me and provide a mount for me.'

He said: 'Where do you stand amongst the young Polytheists?' She had been a singer, who used to sing for the fighters of Quraysh to boost their morale, during their battles with the Prophet.

She said: 'They have not asked me for anything else since the battle of Badr.' So the Apostle of God urged the Bani Abdul-Muttalib to clothe her and provide her with a mount and with funds, which they did. While the Apostle of God was preparing to conquer Mecca, Hatib came to her and gave her the letter and ordered her to take it by a little known route. When Sarah left with the letter, Gabriel descended upon the Apostle of God and told him of this.

The Apostle of God summoned Imam Ali and said to him:

'One of my companions has written a letter to the people of Mecca telling them of our plans. I have already asked God to hide our news from them. The letter is with a woman who has taken it by a different road. So take your sword and catch up with her and take the letter from her. Then let her go and return to me with it. Then he summoned al-Zubeir and said to him: 'Go with Ali ibn Abi Talib on this errand.' So they went and when they caught up with her al-Zubeir said to her: 'Where is the letter you have with you?' But she denied it and swore an oath and wept.

Al-Zubeir said turning to Imam Ali: 'I do not see that she has a letter with her O Abu al-Hasan, so let us return to the Apostle of God and inform him of her innocence.'

Imam Ali said: 'The Apostle of God informs me that she has a letter with her and orders me to take it from her and you tell me that she has no letter with her!'

Then he drew his sword and stepped towards her and said:

'By God you will either produce the letter or I will strike your neck with this sword.' When she saw this earnestness she said: 'If I must do this then at least turn your face away from me O Son of Abu Talib.' So he turned his face from her and she opened her veil and took out the letter from her hair. Then Imam Ali took it and went with it to the Apostle of God.

The affair of Hatib, being as it was, warranted that public opinion be turned against him so that others who were considering acting in a similar manner would be prevented. Perhaps for this reason we see that the Apostle of God ordered that congregational prayers be held and then he ascended the pulpit and took the letter in his hand and said: 'O people, I have asked God to keep information about us from the Quraysh, but a man from amongst you has written to the people of Mecca and told them of our news. So let the owner of the letter rise or revelation will expose him.'

No-one rose so he repeated it and then Hatib ibn Abi Baltaah rose and said: 'O Apostle of God, I wrote the letter but I have not become a hypocrite after my Islam nor have I become a doubter after my certainty.' The Apostle of God said: 'Then what made you write the letter?'

Hatib said seeking an excuse: 'O Apostle of God, I have a family in Mecca but I do not have a tribe that will defend my family, so I wanted to have influence with the people there so that God might defend my family and property. All of the Muhajirin have a tribe there to defend their families and wealth.'

So the Apostle of God excused him and forgave him and said to his companions: 'Do not say anything but kind words to him.' One of the companions said: 'O Apostle of God, let me strike the neck of this hypocrite. He has betrayed God and His Apostle.' The Apostle of God said: 'Leave him.' And he stopped him from attacking Hatib.

Then God revealed the following verses about Hatib:

O you who believe! do not take My enemy and your enemy for friends: would you offer them love while they deny what has come to you of the truth, driving out the Messenger and yourselves because you believe in Allah, your Lord? If you go forth struggling hard in My path

and seeking My pleasure, would you manifest love to
them? And I know what you conceal and what you
manifest; and whoever of you does this, he indeed has
gone astray from the straight path (60:1).
If they find you, they will be your enemies, and will
stretch forth towards you their hands and their tongues
with evil, and they ardently desire that you may
disbelieve. (60:2)
until the verse:

Of no profit to you will be your relatives and your
children on the Day of Resurrection: He will judge
between you, and God sees well all that you do (60:3).
Hatib was forgiven despite his treacherous behaviour of
betraying some of the most sensitive secrets at times of
war, thus blatantly undermining national security.

Before Entering Mecca
Then the Apostle of God ordered al-Abbas to hold Abu
Sufyan - one of the prominent leaders of Quraysh, who
instigated many wars against the prophet, where the
valley narrowed at the front of the mountain where the
soldiers of God would pass by him. This he did and the
tribes passed by him under their banners.

Al-Abbas relates: 'Every time a tribe passed by, Abu
Sufyan would say to me: 'O Abbas, who are they?'

I would say: 'Salim.'

He would say: 'What have I to do with Salim'

Then another tribe would pass by and he would say: 'O Abbas, who are they?'

I would say: 'Muzaynah.'

He would say: 'What have I to do with Muzaynah'. Not a tribe would pass but he would ask me about them and I would inform him of them and he would say: 'What have I to do with such and such a tribe.'

Then the Apostle of God passed by with his detachments including the Muhajirun and the Ansar with eyes of steel.

I said: 'That is the Apostle of God with the Muhajirun and the Ansar.' He said: 'No-one has any capability or power over them.' Then he said: 'I swear, O Abu al-Fadl, the kingdom of your nephew has become great indeed.' I said: 'O Abu Sufyan, this is the Prophethood, (not kingdom).'

Abu Sufyan said: 'Indeed.' Then I said: 'Your people are safe.'

The banner of the Ansar was with Saad ibn Ibadah and when he passed by Abu Sufyan he said to him: 'Today is the day of slaughter, today the women will be captured. O tribes of Aws and Khazraj, this is your revenge for the day of the mountain (Ohud).' Abu Sufyan heard him and kept it to himself until the Apostle of God passed by him when he said: 'Do you know what Saad ibn Ibadah has said? He has said such and such.'

The Apostle of God said: 'What he has said is of no consequence.' Then he sent someone to Saad and took the banner from him and passed it to Imam Ali and said: 'Enter with kindness.' Imam Ali took the banner and began to proclaim: 'Today is the day of mercy, today the honour of the women will be protected.' Then the Apostle of God turned to Abu Sufyan and said to him: 'O Abu Sufyan, proceed to Mecca and let them know of the sanctuary.'

So Abu Sufyan went, until he reached the Quraysh and shouted at the top of his voice: 'O people of Quraysh, here is Muhammad who has come with such force that you cannot contend with. Whoever enters the house of Abu Sufyan has sanctuary and whoever enters the sacred quarter around the Kabah has sanctuary.' They said: 'God slay you! Your house will not save us.' He said: 'And whoever bolts his door has sanctuary.' So the people left for their houses and for the mosque and the Apostle of God proceeded and entered Mecca from the heights.

When the Apostle of God appeared at the pass of Adhakhir, he entered Mecca from that direction. A tent of leather was pitched for him by the grave of his uncle Abu Talib. He refused to reclaim his house or the houses of his companions in Mecca that had been confiscated by the Polytheists.

This was after he had ordered the detachments of his companions and the commanders of his army to surround Mecca completely and to enter by all the

entrances and roads which led to the city from high and
low so that they would block any possibility of
opposition. He ordered them to stay their hands from
fighting and only to fight those who fought them.

He also gave a banner to Abu Ruweihah al-Khathami
and ordered him to proclaim amongst the people of
Mecca:

'Whoever enters under the banner of Abu Ruweihah has
sanctuary.' This was in addition to the three other points
of sanctuary mentioned. So the people were reassured
and threw down their weapons and entered their houses
in safety without anyone being made captive or blood
being spilt.

Then the Prophet visited the Holy House and when he
had finished his circumambulation of the Kabah he went
to the mountain of al-Safa and ascended it. It is said that
he sat in a corner of the mosque such that he looked at
the House. He began to praise God and pray. Then he
called for the custodian of the Kabah who at that time
was Othman ibn Talhah. He had locked the door when
he heard that the Apostle of God had entered Mecca.

He refused to hand over the key so Imam Ali stood up to
him and took the key from him and presented it to the
Apostle of God. He ordered that the door be opened and
he entered and he saw that there were two images inside.
He called for a cloth and made it wet and then erased the
images. Then he prayed two cycles of prayer between
the two pillars upon the red marble. Then he approached

the corners of the House and said 'Allahu Akbar' at each corner.

Then he went to the door of the Kabah and the Quraysh had filled the mosque in rows awaiting to see what he would do with them, assuming - according to the customs of the age of ignorance - that they would be subject to the sword and that they would be exterminated to the last man. But it was not to be like this, for Islam is the way of honor and virtue and the Prophet is the Apostle of mercy and humanism. He took hold of the pillars of the door and made the now famous speech.

The Apostle of God began his speech by praising and extolling God, and said: 'There is no deity but God, no partner has He. He fulfilled His promise and aided His servant and He alone defeated the confederates.'

Then he said: 'Every great deed, or wealth, or claim of blood, or foul deed or feud that existed in the Age of Ignorance are beneath my two feet now. As for the custodianship of the House and the task of watering of the pilgrims, they are returned to their rightful owners. Mecca is sacred by the sanctification of God. None other before me has been allowed free reign therein, and I have only been allowed free reign for a short time on one day. Mecca is sacred until the final hour comes. Trees therein are not to be cut and animals are not to be hunted . . .'

Then he said: 'O people, let those present inform those who are absent that with Islam, God has taken away the

arrogance of the Jahiliyyah and the boasting about
lineage and tribe. All of you are from Adam and Adam
is from clay.'

Then he recited the Qur'anic verse:

O people, We have created you of male and female and
made of you peoples and tribes so that you might know
one another. Surely the most noble amongst you in the
sight of God is the most pious (49:13).
Then he said: 'The best of the servants of God are those
who fear God. Arabic is not a father and sire. but is a
tongue which speaks and if a person's actions do him
down, his lineage will not save him.'
Then he turned to the people of Mecca and said: 'What
foul neighbors to a Prophet you were. You belied and
expelled and tortured my followers and me. Then you
were not satisfied until you came to my lands to fight
me. Now, O people of the Quraysh, what do you say?
What do you think I shall do with you?

They said: 'We think only good and we say only good.
You are a noble brother and the son of a noble brother
and you have defeated us.' The Prophet said: 'I will say
to you what Joseph peace be upon him said to his
brothers:

There is no blame upon you this day, God will forgive
you and He is the Most Merciful (12:92).
Go for ye are at liberty.'

The people left as if they had been raised from their graves, and entered into Islam. God had put the people of Mecca under the Apostle of God's power but because he freed them, the people of Mecca were to become known as the Tulaqa or "those who have been freed".

With The Custodian Of The Kabah

Then the Apostle of God sat in the mosque. Imam Ali came to him bringing the key to the Kabah. Then al-Abbas stood up and asked the Apostle of God to give him the key. At this point the Qur'anic verse was revealed:

Verily God orders you to return all things held in trust to their rightful owners (4:58).

So the Apostle of God ordered Imam Ali to return the key to Othman ibn Talhah. When he did so, Othman ibn Talhah, who did not expect that the key would be returned to him, said: 'O Ali, you took it from me by force and now you return it to me with kindness?' Imam Ali said: 'Yes, for God Almighty has sent down a revelation about you in the Qur'an and has said:

Verily God orders you to return all things held in trust to their rightful owners (4:58).

When 'Othman ibn Talhah heard this he accepted Islam and the Prophet ratified his position as custodian himself. It is also related that Othman ibn Talhah said: 'In the Jahiliyyah we used to open the Kabah on Mondays and Thursdays. One day the Prophet approached and sought to enter the Kabah with some people. This was before he migrated to Medina. But I

locked the door and abused him. He treated me with
kindness and said: 'O Othman, perchance you will one
day see this key in my own hand to do with as I will.

I said: 'That is the day when the Quraysh are destroyed
and humiliated.' He said: 'On the contrary, they will live
and be honored.' Then he entered the Kabah and his
words were such that made me think that they would
come true.

When the day of the conquest of Mecca came he said: 'O
Othman, bring me the key.' But I refused to bring him it.
So Ali took it from me and gave it to him. When he had
completed his prayers and his visit to the House he
returned it to me and said: 'O Othman ibn Talhah, God
has given you custody of His House (the Kabah) so eat
from that which comes to you from this House as is
customary.'

As I was leaving he called me and said: 'Did not what I
say come to pass?'

Then I remembered what he had said to me in Mecca
before the Hijrah and I said: 'Indeed. I bear witness that
you are the Apostle of God.'

Forgive Your Archenemies
The Apostle of God had taken the oath of the Muslims
not to slay in Mecca anyone other than those who fought
them, with the exception of a few who were harming the
Prophet and those who entered Islam with him, and who
were inciting war and fighting against him and

preventing the people from the way of God and the truth. These included the likes of Habbar ibn al-Aswad who had attacked Zainab the (step) daughter of the Apostle of God when she was migrating and terrorized her which caused the miscarriage of her child and an illness of which she died. Another of them was Ikrimah ibn Abi Jahl who was one of the inciters of wars and those who fanned the flames of dissent against the Muslims. There were also two songstresses who used to sing mocking the Apostle of God and incited the Polytheists against him on the day of the battle of Ohud. These people went into hiding.

News reached Imam Ali that two of them who were the relatives of Umm Hani the sister of Imam Ali had sought sanctuary with Umm Hani and she had granted it to them in her house. Imam Ali went to her house wearing an iron helmet, which masked his face and called: 'Send out those you are protecting.' The two men were terrified and Umm Hani feared for their safety. Umm Hani went out to him not knowing who he was and said: 'O servant of God, I am Umm Hani the daughter of the uncle of the Apostle of God and the sister of Ali ibn Abi Talib so leave my house.

Imam Ali said: 'Send them out.'

She said: 'I swear that I will complain to the Apostle of God about you.' Imam Ali took off the helmet and she recognized him and approached him and said: 'May I be your sacrifice, I swore to complain of you to the Apostle of God.'

He said to her: 'Go and make good your oath. He is at the top of the valley.' So she came to him distressed and when the Apostle of God had heard her story he said: 'Welcome O Umm Hani, we give sanctuary to those you have given sanctuary to.'

As for Habbar, he fled then he accepted Islam and he was pardoned.

The Apostle of God was asked for pardon for Sarah and one of the lady singers, which he granted and they entered Islam.

As for Ibn Abi Sarh, he entered Islam and was brought by Othman who asked the Apostle of God for pardon which was granted. He had entered Islam before this then he migrated to Medina where he turned away from Islam and returned to Mecca.

Most of the people that the Apostle of God had called for their deaths were given sanctuary after other people interceded on their behalf so they came out from their hiding places. Then they came to the Apostle of God and entered Islam and he accepted their Islam and pardoned them.

One of these people were Safwan ibn Omayyah who had fled. Omeir ibn Wahab al-Jumahi sought sanctuary for him from the Apostle of God, which he granted and he gave him the turban, which he had been wearing when he entered Mecca.

Omeir caught up with Safwan as he was about to set off
to sea and he stopped him and said: 'O Safwan,
remember God lest you perish. I have brought the
sanctuary of the Apostle of God.' Safwan was sceptical,
and said: 'Go away and do not speak to me.'

Omeir who wanted to convince him said: 'O Safwan, I
tell you that the most virtuous of people and the most
pious of people and the best of people is your cousin.
His might is your might and his honor is your honor and
his wealth is your wealth.'

Safwan: 'I fear for myself from him.'

Omeir said to him: 'He is not as you imagine, he is more
clement and noble than that.' Safwan was convinced
when Omeir showed him the Apostle of God's turban
which he had sent as a sign of his sanctuary. So he
returned with him and when they stood before the
Apostle of God Safwan said: 'This man claims that you
have granted me an amnesty.' The Prophet said: 'He has
spoken truly.'

He said: 'Then give me two months to make up my
mind.' The Prophet said: 'You have four months.' Also
among those who sought and were granted amnesty by
the Apostle of God was [the prophet's prominent
adversary] Ikrimah ibn Abi Jahl whose wife Umm
Hakim daughter of al-Harith ibn Hisham sought amnesty
for him. She informed him: 'I have come to you from the
most pious and best of people. Do not throw yourself

into perdition for I have sought amnesty for you and it was granted.' So he went with her to the Apostle of God and accepted Islam at his hands then he said: 'O Apostle of God, show me the best of what you know so that I may learn it.'

He said: 'Say: 'There is no deity but God and Muhammad is the servant and Apostle of God, then strive in the way of God.'

With His Would Be Assassin
It is reported that Fadalah ibn Omeir ibn al-Mulawwwah sought to kill the Apostle of God while he was walking round the Kabah - the symbolic House of God in the holy city of Mecca. When he drew near to him the Apostle of God said:

'Is it Fadalah?' He said: 'Yes.' The Prophet said: 'What are you contemplating about?' He said: 'Nothing, I was contemplating about God.' The Prophet laughed and said: 'Ask God for forgiveness.' Then the Prophet put his hand on Fadalah's chest and the latter's heart became calm. Fadalah used to say: 'I swear that no sooner had he raised his hand from my chest than he was the most beloved to me of all God's creation.' It was through such noble morals and fine conduct that the people came to accept Islam in droves.

Abandoning The Prophet's Teachings
Among those who were sent by the Apostle of God after the conquest of Mecca to invite the people to God was

Khalid ibn al-Walid who was sent to the Judheimah tribe as a missionary and not to fight them.

When Khalid and his men stopped at a well of the Judheimah tribe at al-Ghumeisa', the Judheimah took up their weapons and said: 'O Khalid, we have not taken up our weapons against God and His Apostle while we are Muslims. So look carefully. If the Apostle of God has sent you as a raider then here are our camels and our flocks for you to fall upon.'

Khalid said: 'Leave your weapons.' They said: 'We fear that you will take us for the feud of the Jahiliyyah when God and His Apostle have laid the feuds of the Jahiliyyah to rest.'13 Khalid and his men left them and stopped close by. Then he attacked them with his horsemen and killed and captured some men. Khalid ordered that they be bound then he put them to the sword.

Treachery And Making Amends
When Khalid had betrayed the Judheimah their messenger came to the Apostle of God and informed him of what Khalid had done to them. The Apostle of God raised his hands to the heavens after he had ascended the pulpit and told the people of what Khalid had done and said: 'O God, I distance myself from what Khalid ibn al-Walid has done.' He repeated this declaration three times, and wept.

Then he summoned Imam Ali and gave him some gold that he had with him and said: 'O Ali, go to the

Judheimah and look into the matter and satisfy them for what Khalid has done.' Then he raised his feet and said: 'O Ali, let the judgements of the Jahiliyyah be under your feet.' When Imam Ali reached them he judged according to the judgement of God Almighty and when he returned to the Prophet, the Apostle of God said: 'O Ali, tell me of what you have done.'

Imam Ali said to him: 'O Apostle of God, I went there and gave the compensation for every blood spilt, and for every foetus lost, and for all property [that was damaged or looted]. I found I had a surplus so I compensated them for their dogs' water pots, . . . and for the fear their women felt and the terror their children had (as a result of the attack) and for the things that they may be aware of as well as for those they may not. Then I still found I had a surplus so I gave to them so that they would be pleased with you O Apostle of God.'

At this the Apostle of God who looked well pleased said: 'O Ali, you gave to them so that they would be pleased with me, may God be pleased with you.'

Then he said: 'O Ali, you to me have the station of Aaron had to Moses except that there would be no prophet after me. O Ali, you are the guide of my nation. The truly blessed is he who loves you and follows your way and the truly wretched is he who hates you and neglects your way until the Day of Judgement.'16

Chapter 4:
Social Policies Of Prophet Muhammad.

The Messenger of Allah remained constantly on the road, touring the districts of Medina, visiting domiciled tribes, meeting with people, providing them with guidance, leading them in prayers at their mosques and at his own mosque, visiting their sick, walking behind their coffins during their funeral processions and delegating the responsibilities of the state and the nation, to whoever he wanted from among his companions.

He appointed for the women a virtuous lady named Umm Waraqah to lead their prayers. Women who wanted to offer prayers used to go to the house of Umm Waraqah to pray with her. He also built in Medina about fifty other mosques. He paid a great deal of attention to construction in Medina after it became completely Muslim, urging people to build and to construct.

He invited the Bedouins surrounding Medina to migrate and settle there and to abandon their migratory habits. Many Bedouins went and resided in Medina, becoming members of the Islamic nation. Their settlements became the center for migrants and they made alliances with whomever they wanted from among the tribes of the Ansar. Many of them entered into an alliance with the Messenger of Allah and with Bani Hashim.

Medina expanded and its population increased. People started cultivating the vast lands in the valley without anyone to deter them or to stop them, and there was no tax on construction or agriculture. Historians have mentioned that the number of the Muslims from among the residents of Medina increased by a third before the battle of the Khandaq (moat) and doubled thereafter.

The Messenger of Allah wrote a document for the Muhajirun and the Ansar making the residents of each quarter responsible for their quarter in particular and for the security of the city in general. Thus, it was a popular government whose reins were in the hands of the people themselves, and the settlement of anyone who migrated to Medina was done upon that basis. The Messenger of Allah used to distribute to the Muslims whatever he obtained of the charity, zakat, khums, donations and occasionally booty.

The Prophet also made large quarters in his Mosque where homeless people could stay. According to some historical records, the number of those residents reached four hundred. They formed part of the army of the Prophet during war time, stood in rows behind him whenever he led the congregational prayers, sat under his pulpit whenever he delivered sermons and conveyed his orders to other Muslims as needed. The Messenger of Allah used to gradually help them get married and get them to acquire housing and means of earning a living and the like. People sensed the bliss of Islam, so they remained on its path.

Medina enjoyed a measure of prosperity that no other area of the Arabian Peninsula had ever known before, nor did the world ever before come to know such a government. Chosroe and Caesar's governments and the like were distant from people, arrogant towards them, not mixing with them. They used to levy huge taxes, rule the people as despots, plundering their wealth, causing poverty, diseases, ignorance and chaos prevailed in their lands.

However, the government ruling Medina and its suburbs was an ideal one. Although historians have documented the events taking place during the Prophet's time, we never heard about crimes or disputes except rarely. The role model of the Prophet was present in people's minds, and they used to emulate it; so, there was no need for a police force or an executive power, usury, monopoly, or taxes other than zakat1 or jizya2 or khiraj3. Everything was administered very well; therefore, we do not find in the history of Medina that there were complaints about chaos or the absence of law and order.

The Islamic legislative system benefits everyone and equates everyone, giving the nation true power, peace of mind, stability, firmness and progress. People's belief in lofty Islamic ideals, represented in the person of the Prophet, prevailed on everything.

It is obvious that in such an environment, personal problems and disputes are minimized, and people are overwhelmed by the spirit of togetherness, adopting the trend of giving, generosity, avoiding falling into prohibitions and sins such as theft, rape, adultery, murder, sodomy, backbiting and other such crimes. People demonstrated beautiful manners, which had hitherto never been known, whether throughout the Arabian Peninsula or anywhere else then.

People used to favor others over their own selves in giving in the cause of Allah Almighty. One favored his friend over himself as far as wealth was concerned. The incident involving the Commander of the Faithful Imam Ali and his family, wherein the verse saying -

And they feed the poor, the orphan and the captive, (76:8).
for the love of God, (saying,) We feed you for the sake of God alone: We desire no reward from you, nor thanks. (76:9).
We only fear a Day of distressing Wrath from our Lord (76:10).
is a glorious example.

One would inquire about the wellbeing of his neighbor and his family before inquiring about their own, and wealthy people used to provide aid and food for those who needed it without being asked for help. The Prophet did not need to force or coerce anyone nor did he confiscate anyone's wealth, nor did he kill anyone arbitrarily. News of the new community continued to reverberate throughout the Arabian Peninsula and throughout surrounding countries, which claimed to have deeply rooted civilizations – this was the community about which the Holy Qur'an said:

You are the best nation sent to people (3:110). Everyone felt that a new era had dawned, so all hearts were attracted to Islam and people rallied behind it willingly and obediently. Thus, tribes, countries and groups hostile to Islam yielded before the Messenger of Allah on account of the popularity of his government and the freedom of the people, blended with conviction, virtue, piety, cooperation and love for everything good.

As part of his socio-economic policy on welfare and inheritance the Prophet used to say, "He who dies and leaves poor family behind, then they should come to me for I am responsible for them and their welfare."Then he went further with monetary policy and said, "One who dies and leaves a bequest, it belongs to his family. And whoever dies leaving a debt behind, I am responsible for it."4

The Prophet was extremely humble, a man who mended his own sandals, patched his clothes, milked his she-camel, served his family lovingly. He loved the poor and the indigent, sat with them, visited their sick, and never insulted anyone who fell into poverty on account of his poverty nor venerated anyone wealthy on account of his wealth. He always accepted another's excuse, never dealt with anyone in a way which the latter did not like, walked with widows and with slaves, never feared kings nor rulers, and never despised the weak. He always walked behind his companions saying, "Let me turn my back only to the angels", and sometimes he walked in their midst.

He always responded to whoever invited him, accepted any present, even if it were a trotter meal, and he rewarded the giver. He would only become angry with regards to the breaches of the commands of his Lord but never for himself. He was easygoing, lenient, neither harsh nor rough, nor was he boisterous, nor profane, nor pointing out people's faults, nor was he a flatterer.

He overlooked whatever he disliked and always gave hope to whoever asked him for something. Nobody feared evil as coming from him, but everyone expected good to come from him. One of his servants has narrated saying, "I was in the service of the Messenger of Allah for ten years. Never did he ever complain to me, nor did he ever ask me why I did or did not do this or that."

It was his habit to respond to those who called upon him with the very best of response. Whoever called him, he would respond with the words "At your service"

Jurayr ibn Abdullah is quoted as having said, "The Messenger of Allah never put a barrier before me since I accepted Islam. Whenever he saw me, he smiled. He used to joke with his companions, socialize with them, talk with them, tease their children and seat them in his lap, and he used to respond to anyone who invited him, visit the sick even if they lived in distant parts of the city, accept everyone's apology and never put himself above anyone, including his servants, be it with regard to what he ate or wore."

He used to ride the camel, the mare or the mule, and used to tie a stone on his stomach on account of the pangs of hunger. He always initiated whoever he met with his greeting of peace, prolonged his prayers whenever he prayed alone, but whenever he led others in the congregational prayers, he shortened it out of his concern for the convenience of those whom he led. He used to make his sermons on Fridays and on other occasions brief so that the people would not be bored.

He used to be a friend of men of dignity, dealing generously with those of distinction, being humorous and never saying anything but the truth. Whenever he was assaulted and exposed to hardships because of the ignorant people, he used to say, "Lord! I plead to You to guide my people, for they do not know."He did not invoke the Almighty's wrath against them.

When his molar teeth were broken and he was wounded in the face, it was extremely hard for his companions to see him in that state, so they said, "O Messenger of Allah! Why don't you pray against them?"he said, "I was not sent to curse; rather, I was sent as a Caller – to call people to God and as a Mercy. Lord! I plead to You to guide my people, for they do not know!"

Thus, he did not content himself by simply remaining silent while facing their mischief but forgave them, demonstrated compassion towards them, prayed for them and sought an excuse for them when he said that they did not know any better, just like a kind and compassionate father.

Some of his companions narrated saying that he was once wearing a mantle with coarse edges and a Bedouin pulled him very hard, so much so that the edges left their marks on his shoulder. Then the Bedouin said, "O Muhammad! Load for me on these two camels of mine with the wealth of Allah which you have for you will not be loading for me anything of your own wealth nor the wealth of your father."

The Prophet remained silent for a moment then said, "The wealth belongs to Allah and I am His servant; O Bedouin! Shall I seek retribution for what you have done to me?"The Bedouin said, "No."He said, "Why not?"The Bedouin said, "It is so because you do not reward evil with evil."The Prophet smiled then ordered barley to be loaded for him on one camel and dates on another.

The Prophet's people harmed him in many ways; they spat on his face, emptied sheep's stomach over his head, knocked him to the ground and trampled on his back, put thorns in his path, confiscated his property, exiled him, conspired against him, killed his uncle, step-daughter, step-granddaughter, ridiculed him, called him a wizard, possessed, insane, a poet, a priest upon whom the wrath of some of their gods had befallen. This was in addition to causing other types of harm, so much so that he said, "No prophet has been harmed as much as I have been."

Yet he remained patient in the face of such hardships till Allah granted him the upper hand over them, placing him in charge of their affairs while they had no doubt that they would be uprooted, their community annihilated, and their wealth confiscated.

After the fall of Mecca, he did not go beyond forgiving and overlooking the harm dealt to him by the Meccans to whom he said, "What do you think I am going to do to you?"They said, "You will deal with us with kindness. You are a gracious brother and the son of a gracious brother."The Prophet said, "I shall say to you just as my brother the Prophet Joseph had said: 'No harm upon you; go, for you are free'". Thus he forgave all of them, including the most bitter of his enemies such as Abu Sufyan and Hind.

He forgave men like Ikrimah ibn Abu Jahl who was similar to his father in his harming of the Messenger of Allah and in his animosity, spending a great deal on fighting him, like Safwan ibn Omayyah ibn Khalaf who was very cruel to the Prophet and who used to finance the armies of the polytheists – he was a man who could be called in today's terminology the "Minister of Defense"for the infidels.

The Prophet forgave men like Habbar ibn al-Aswad who terrorized Zainab, his stepdaughter, causing her to miscarry, and consequently died after falling ill. The Messenger of Allah had permitted anyone to kill him.

When the man came to know that the Prophet was used
to forgiving criminals, he went to him seeking his
forgiveness, apologizing for his ill deeds. He said, "We,
O Prophet of Allah, used to associate partners with
Allah, but Allah Almighty guided us through you, saving
us from perdition; so, do forgive my ignorance and
forgive what you are told about me, for I do admit the
evil of my actions and confess my sins."

The Messenger of Allah said to him, "I have forgiven
you, and Allah has fared very well with you since He
guided you to Islam, and Islam cancels whatever
precedes it."

The Prophet also forgave Wahshi, killer of Hamzah - the
beloved uncle and partisan of the Prophet. It is narrated
that Wahshi, embraced Islam and then went to the
Messenger of Allah after feeling secure from his wrath.
The Prophet said to him, "O Wahshi!"He said,
"Yes!"The Prophet said, "Tell me, how did you kill my
uncle?"Wahshi told him how, and he wept, then he
forgave him.

He also forgave Hind despite her numerous crimes.5 The
Prophet forgave men like Abdullah ibn al-Zubari who
used to lampoon the Messenger of Allah, speaking ill of
him and of the Muslims. When Mecca fell in the hands
of the Muslims, he fled, and when he came to know that
Muhammad was a merciful and humane Messenger of
Allah, he returned to him and apologized. The
Messenger of Allah accepted his apology, so the man

accepted Islam and composed the following poetic
verses:

I apologize to you for what I did
When in misguidance I aimlessly was lost,
So forgive me, may both my parents be
For your sake be offered as a sacrifice.
Forgive my slippage for you give mercy
And upon you did mercy descend,
And I have already testified that your creed
Is truly the right creed and that you are
Among God's servants, great indeed.

Amongst the several assassination attempts made on the
Prophet's life, a Jewish woman made one. However, the
Prophet forgave the Jewess who served him with
poisoned sheep's meat. The Prophet sought her, and she
admitted it.

Imam al-Baqir has said, "The Messenger of Allah
summoned the Jewess who served him poisoned meat
from sheep and said to her, 'What prompted you to do
what you did?' She said, 'I said to myself that if he truly
is a Prophet, it would not harm him, but if he seeks
authority, I would relieve people of him.' The Messenger
of Allah, then, forgave her and let her go.

The Prophet used to say, "Allah taught me good manners
and I taught Ali. My Lord ordered me to be generous
and kind and forbade me from being miserly or mean.
There is nothing Allah hates more than miserliness and
bad manners which ruin one's good deeds just as vinegar

ruins honey."He used to spend everything he had by way of charity till he and his family would be bitten by hunger.

Imam al-Sadiq has narrated saying that the Messenger of Allah went to al-Jirana and distributed the booty of Honain there, which was quite large. People kept asking him, and he kept giving them until they pushed him against a tree, stripped him of his garment and caused the tree to severely scratch his back. They still kept asking him for a share until they had removed him from there. He then said to them, "O people! Give me back my garment for by Allah, had I any wealth, I would have distributed it among you, and you know full well that I am neither a coward nor a miser."

He said the following to his uncle Abbas during the time when he was sick and shortly before his demise, "O uncle of the Messenger of Allah! Do you accept to carry my will, make all preparations for my funeral and pay my debts on my behalf?"Abbas said, "O Messenger of Allah! Your uncle is an old man who has many dependents to take care of and you compete with the wind in your swiftness of generosity and open-handedness and you have a debt which is beyond your uncle's means."

The Messenger of Allah, as historians have recorded, used to give whenever he was asked, and when he did not have anything to give, he would make a promise of payment. Since his uncle refused to accept to carry out his will, he asked Ali to do that instead, and Ali assented and carried out the will of the Prophet.

Jabir ibn Abdullah al-Ansari has said, "The Messenger of Allah never said 'No' to anyone who made a request of him."

There have been quite a few incidents narrated when a man would approach him requesting something and he would say to him, "I do not have what you are asking me for, but if we get something, we shall give it to you."

A man once asked him for something, and he did not have anything to give him, and some of his companions were present. The latter said, "O Messenger of Allah! Allah never required you to do what you cannot."Another companion responded to this comment and said, "O Messenger of Allah! Spend of what there is with you and do not fear that the One Who has the Throne will ever disappoint you."The Prophet smiled and signs of pleasure were seen on his face.

Earn Your Living

It is related that Imam Ja'far al-Sadiq said: 'Never was the Apostle of God asked by anyone for some worldly thing without him giving it. Once a woman sent him her son and said to him: 'Go to him and ask from him. If he says I have nothing then say to him: 'Give me your shirt.' The boy did what his mother had ordered him. The Apostle of God took off his shirt and gave it to him.'

With A Jew

The Commander of the Faithful is reported to have said, "The Messenger of Allah owed a Jew some money that came one day to collect them. The Messenger of Allah said to him, 'O Jew! I do not have it.' The Jew said, 'O Muhammad! I am not going to part with you till you pay me back.'

The man confined the Messenger of Allah there and then till the Prophet had performed the noon, afternoon, sunset and evening prayers and went beyond that until he prayed the morning prayer of the following day as well. The companions of the Messenger of Allah kept threatening that Jew. The Messenger of Allah looked at them and said, 'What are you going to do to him?' They said, 'O Messenger of Allah! How dare a Jew to confine you like that?' He said, 'My Lord, the most Exalted and the Greatest, did not send me to oppress anyone with whom I have entered into an agreement nor anyone else.'

Some half of the day had passed away, when the Jew said, 'I testify that there is no god but Allah and that Muhammad is His servant and Messenger; and half of my wealth I shall give away in the way of Allah.'"

Since the Prophet was always moving around, checking about the different quarters of the city, he used to assign someone to succeed him in performing the prayers at the Mosque whenever he went elsewhere. It seems that the above incident took place at one of the quarters, which he was checking.

He never ignored anyone's need even if she were a bondmaid, nor did he sit leaning on some support, nor did he ever gaze at anyone, and he always accepted presents, even as little a present as a drink of milk.

Some of his companions have narrated that if he missed any of his brethren for three days, he would inquire about him; so, if he was away, he prayed for him; if he was present, he went to visit him; if he was sick, he would pay him a visit. He did not let anyone walk with him if he himself was riding till he let him ride with him. If the man refused, he would say to him, "Go ahead of me and join me at the place which you seek."

He used to help his companions as if he was one of them without reflecting an attitude of superiority to them in anything small or big. He was once travelling, when He ordered a sheep to be prepared for food. A man said, "O Messenger of Allah! I shall undertake slaughtering it."Another said, "I shall skin it."Another said, "I shall cook it."He said, "And I shall gather the firewood."They said to him, "We all can spare you the trouble."He said, "I know that you can spare me the trouble, but I do not want to have any distinction over you, for Allah hates to see His servant receiving a special treatment from his companions,"then he went and gathered some firewood.

He was once on a trip when he alighted to perform the prayers, but then returned. It was said to him, "O Messenger of Allah! What do you wish to do?"He said, "I want to tie my she-camel."They said, "We will tie it for you.""No,"he said, "None of you should exploit others, not even for a small piece of a tooth stick."(short lengths of twigs used as toothbrushes.)

An envoy sent by the Negus visited the Prophet in Medina; so the Prophet stood up to personally tend to them. His companions said to him, "O Messenger of Allah! We can spare you the trouble!"He said to them, "They showered our folks with their generosity, so I would love to reward them likewise."

Whenever Prophet listened to someone, he would never turn his face away from him till the person himself did so. Whenever he shook hands with someone, he would not pull his hand away till the other person did. He never stood up after having sat with someone till the latter himself stood up, and would initiate anyone who met him with his greeting, including the children and the women, and he was the one to initiate shaking hands with his companions.

He used to shower his generosity on whoever visited him, so much so that he would even spread his outer mantle for him to sit on, or offered him to sit on his mat instead. He used to choose nicknames for his companions in order to honor them, calling them by the names, which they loved the most. And he would never interrupt anyone.

Salman narrated once saying, "I entered once the house of the Messenger of Allah and found him leaning on a pillow. He placed it for me saying, 'O Salman! No

Muslim receives a Muslim brother, and places a pillow for him out of respect, except that Allah forgives him. ' "

If Prophet was performing his prayers and someone came to see him, he would shorten his prayers so that he could finish quickly and help the man. Once he was through with helping the man, he would go back to his prayers. He used to smile the most and his breath was surely the very best of all.

Those who used to serve the residents of Medina used to go to see the Messenger of God during early morning prayers, taking their pots of water with them to him so he might dip his hand in the water and thus bless it. He used to dip his hand in each pot, and someone could even bring a pot of very cold water, yet the Messenger of God did not mind and he would still dip his hand in it.

Usually a small child would be brought to him so that he could bless him. He would pray for him to be blessed, or he would choose a name for him or recite the Adhan (call to prayer) in his ears. He would take the child and place him in his lap as a sign of respect for his family. Occasionally a child would urinate on him, causing some of those present to rebuke the child. But he would say, "Do not thus hurt the feelings of the child."He would leave the child till the latter had fully relieved himself, then he would then finish his prayers for him, or choose a name for him or recite the call to prayer in his ears. All of this caused the child's family to be very happy when they noticed how he was not offended.

Once they were gone, the Prophet would wash his clothes.

If anyone sat near him, he would move a little to make room for him. Once a man said to him, "O Messenger of Allah! There is plenty of room in the place."He said, "Yes, but a Muslim is obligated, when another Muslim sits near him, to move a little as a sign of respect for him."

He Endeavoured To Please Others
Prophet Mohammad never left anyone without pleasing him. It has been recorded that a Bedouin once came to ask him for something. He gave it to him then said, "Have I done good to you?"The Bedouin said, "No, you have not, nor have you done anything nice for me."The Muslims present there were very angry with that man, and they stood up to warn him, but the Prophet asked them to stay away.

Then he stood up and entered inside his home and called the man to him, giving him some more. Then he asked him again, "Have I now done something good for you?"The Bedouin said, "Yes, may Allah reward you goodness that encompasses your family and tribe."The Prophet said to him, "What you have said earlier, has resulted in something from inside in hearts of my companions; so, if you like, go back to them and tell them what you have just told me so that what is in their hearts against you will go away."The Bedouin assented.

Later on, the Prophet came and said, "This Bedouin said what he said, so we gave him an increase till he has felt pleased. Is not that so?"The Bedouin said, "Yes; may Allah reward you goodness that encompasses your family."

Then the Prophet said to his companions, "My example and that of this man is one whose she-camel fled away from him, so people pursued her, causing her to be more rebellious, so her owner called upon them to leave him and his she-camel alone, since he was more kind to her than them. He went to her, took her back and mounted on her. Had I left you alone to deal with this Bedouin on account of what he had said, he would have been dead by now."

If anyone misbehaved towards him, he used to respond to him in a beautiful way. Al-Ala ibn al-Hadrami has been quoted as having asked the Prophet saying, "I have a family whose members, when I am good to them, they reward me with evil, and when I maintain good ties with them, they sever their ties from me."The Messenger of Allah, reciting a Qur'anic verse, said,

Repel (evil) with that which is fairer and behold, he between whom and thee there is enmity shall be as if he were a loyal friend (41:34).
It is related that Imam Ja'far al-Sadiq said: 'One of the companions of the Apostle of God was in dire circumstances. His wife said to him: 'If only you would go to the Prophet and ask from him.' So the man went to the Prophet and when he saw him the Prophet said:

'Whoever asks from us then we will give to him and whoever seeks independent means then God will make him independent.'
The man said to himself: 'He means none other than me.' So he went to his wife and told her. She said: 'The Apostle of God is surely a human being so let him know of our circumstances.' So the man went to the Prophet once again and when the Prophet saw him he said: 'Whoever asks from us then we will give to him and whoever seeks independent means then God will make him independent.'

The man did this for a third time after which he went and borrowed an axe and went to the mountains. There he climbed and began to cut firewood which he brought down and sold for half a measure of flour. He took this home and ate it. The next day he brought down even more firewood and sold it. He continued to do this until he was able to buy an axe.

Then he kept gathering until he was able to buy two young camels and a servant after which he became rich and his life became easy. He went to the Prophet and told him how he had come to ask from him and how he had heard the Prophet speaking. The Prophet said: 'I said to you: 'Whoever asks us then we will give to him and whoever seeks independent means then God will make him independent.'

A narrative states that a Bedouin from Banu Salim came to the Messenger of Allah, stood in front of him and called upon him saying, "O Muhammad! O Muhammad! You are a lying sorcerer, more lying than any other that there is under the shade or in the plains! You are the one who claims that in this green land you have a God Who sent you to the black and to the white! I swear by the idols of Lat and Ozza that had I not feared my folks describing me as rash, I would have hit you with this sword of mine one blow that will kill you, thus making myself the master of the first generations and of the last!"

One of the companions leapt up to hit him, but the Prophet said to the companion, "Sit down; a clement person is almost as good as a prophet."Then the Messenger of Allah turned to the Bedouin and said, "O brother of Banu Salim! Is this how Arabs behave?! They approach us at our place of meeting and then assail us with such rough language?! O Bedouin! I swear by the One Who sent me as a Prophet with the truth, anyone who harms me in the life of this world shall be tomorrow in the fire, being tormented."

The Bedouin, who expected a similar rash response from the Prophet, was moved by the latter's clemency and the overlooking of his own harsh words. He paused and contemplated on the manner and behaviour of the Prophet in response to his words, and upon his reminder of the hereafter, and the values that he held dear. The Bedouin began to realize the virtue and magnanimity of the Prophet of Islam.

After some soul searching, the man accepted Islam and thereafter started inviting his tribesmen to Islam, until the Muslim population amongst his tribe numbered more than five hundred.

The Quraysh kept admitting the Prophet's truthfulness, trustworthiness and every virtue. Even when al-Akhnas met Abu Jahl8 during the battle of Badr and said to him, "O Abu al-Hakam! Only you and I are here; nobody hears our dialogue, could you please inform me about Muhammad, is he truthful or a liar?"Abu Jahl said, "By Allah! Muhammad is truthful; never has Muhammad ever told a lie."

Heraclius asked Abu Sufyan, who was one of the Prophet's archenemies, about him saying, "Did you all accuse him of telling lies even before his claim that he is what he says he is?"Abu Sufyan answered with a simple "No".

One of his wives has narrated saying that a Jew entered the house of the Messenger of Allah and said, "As-Samm Alaik (death be upon you)!"Another Jew entered and repeated the same. The wife became angry and responded, "Alaikumis-Samm wal Ghadab wal Laana (death be upon you, and Divine Wrath and Curse)". The Messenger of Allah then said to her, "Had verbal abuse been an example, it would have been a bad example; never was kindness placed on anything except that it beautified it, and it was never removed from anything except that it stained it."

When his foster sister, whose name was Shayma, came
to visit him once, he spread his outer mantle for her and
seated her on it. Then he said to her, "If you wish, you
can stay with me surrounded with honors and love, or I
can provide you with rations and you may return to your
people."She chose to return to her folks; therefore, he
gave her some money and she returned very pleased.

He was sitting once when a woman came and got close
to him. He stood up for her, spread his own outer mantle
for her, so she sat on it. His companions asked each
other who that woman was. They said that she was the
woman who had nursed him."

It has been narrated that he was once sitting when his
foster father came, so he put his own outer mantle for
him to sit on. Then his foster mother came, so he seated
her on it too. Then his foster brother came, so the
Messenger of Allah seated him in front of him.

Out of to his kindness and loyalty, he used to send some
money and clothes to Thawbiyya - bondmaid of Abu
Lahab - the woman who had nursed him when he was a
baby. When she died, he asked, "Who from among her
relatives is still alive?"He intended to send something to
her relatives, but he was told that she had no living
relatives.

He quite often remembered Khadijah after she had died,
slaughtered a she-camel then send the meat as presents
to her friends out of his devotion to her.

Khadijah had said to him once, "O Messenger of Allah! Good news! By Allah, Allah shall never expose you to shame; for you always visit your relatives, are generous to your guest, and you offer solace during calamities."

Whenever he entered a gathering, he would sit in the nearest available space, and he used to sit on the floor and eat on the ground. As he did, he would say, "I am a slave of Allah; I eat as slaves do, and I sit as a slave sits."

A woman with a sharp tongue once saw him sitting at a mountain's foot, so she said to him, "O Muhammad! By Allah! You eat as slaves eat and you sit as a slave sits." The Messenger of Allah said, "Is there a more dedicated slave of Allah than I am?"

Imam al-Sadiq said the following in his description of the Messenger of Allah: "He used to prefer to ride on the donkey without a saddle, eat while sitting on the most modest of all types of flooring in the company of the slaves, handing something to the beggar in his own hand. He used to ride a donkey and seat his slave or anyone else behind him. He used to ride a mare, a mule or a donkey without any hesitation."

On the day the Muslims scored a victory over Bani Quraydha, he was riding a donkey whose reins were made of cable made of leaves of a date-tree. It was possible for the Prophet to ride the best of the horses, for hundreds were available to his forces, but he opted for a humble way of life and preferred to be like the majority

of people at that time who could not afford more than a
donkey as a means of transport.

In an incident, Imam al-Baqir is quoted as having said,
"The Messenger of Allah walked out seeking to take
care of an errand. He saw al-Fadhl ibn al-Abbas so he
said, "Let this youth ride behind me,"then the Messenger
of Allah rode on with his hand behind the youth. Then
he said to the youth, "Young man! Fear Allah, you will
then find Him before you. O young man! Fear Allah and
He shall make you independent of anyone else."

Whenever he went home, he kept busy doing home
chores, helping his wife, cutting the meat, and sitting
most humbly to eat his meal. He used to lick his fingers
but never belched. He milked his sheep, patched his torn
shirt, mended his sandals and took care of his needs.

He used to feed and tie his camel, feed his animals, take
a bath by himself at night, give company to the poor, eat
with the indigent, handing food over to them in person.
He used to judge justly, make decisive decisions, so both
his foes and friends loved him. And he was trustworthy,
loyal, truthful, so much so that prior to his prophetic
mission, his people used to call him "al- Amin,"the
trustworthy one.

It has been narrated that when the Prophet wanted to
migrate from Mecca to Medina as a result of the
persecution at the hands of the Quraysh, he left Imam
Ali behind him to pay his debts and to return the trusts

with which he had been entrusted with by his foes. He did not say that he was fleeing away from those people's evil because they sought to kill him, so their wealth was lawful for him to take because they were infidels who were fighting him.

Prophet Mohammad had these qualities since before the start of his prophetic mission. It is reported that, in the pre-Islamic times, when they completed the reconstruction of the Kabah, the various tribes of Quraysh disputed with each other with regard to who would put the Black Stone in its place. They decided that the first person to enter their meeting place would be the one to do it.

It was then that the Prophet entered, and this took place before the mission of Prophethood. They, therefore, said, "Here is Muhammad, the Trustworthy one! We accept his arbitration!"In order to please everyone involved and that no one would be left out, Muhammad instructed them to bring a large cloth, spread it on the ground, place the Black Stone on the cloth, and invited one member of every tribe to grab a corner of this cloth and lift it to the level of the place of the Black Stone, and thus he positioned it in its place.

An incident testifying to his fulfilment of his promise says that Ammar said, "I used to tend to cattle before the advent of Islam, and so did Muhammad. I said once to him, 'O Muhammad! Would you like to go to Fakhkh to let the cattle graze there, for I left it when there was lightning in the sky - a harbinger of rain and, thus pasture?' He agreed. So I went there the next day, only to find Muhammad already there, trying to keep his flock away from the pasture. He said to me, 'I had promised you to be there, so I hated to give my flock access to the pasture before you.'"

The Pragmatic Statesman
Prophet Mohammad was lenient, always looking for the best ways to reach reconciliation, and peace. In the process of signing the peace treaty of Hodaybiyah, the Messenger of Allah invited Ali ibn Abu Talib and said to him, "Write: In the Name of Allah, the most Gracious, the most Merciful."Quraysh's envoy, Suhayl, objected saying, "As for 'the most Gracious,' by Allah, I do not know who He is. Rather, you should write: 'In Thy Name, O Lord!' instead."

The Muslims said, "By Allah! We shall not write it except In the Name of Allah, the most Gracious, the most Merciful."

The Prophet said to Ali "Write: 'In Thy Name, O Lord.'"Then he went on to say to Ali, "Following is what Muhammad, the Messenger of Allah, has decided."Suhayl objected again by saying, "Had we recognized you as the Messenger of Allah, we would not have kept you away from the House of Allah, nor would we have fought you. Rather, write your name as Muhammad son of Abdullah."

The Prophet said, "I am the Messenger of Allah even if you accuse me of lying."Then the Messenger of Allah asked Ali to erase the phrase saying "the Messenger of Allah", but Ali refused to do so, so the Prophet took the sheet and erased the phrase himself. Then Ali replaced it with "Muhammad son of Abdullah"instead.

The Messenger of Allah had come to the enlightened city of Medina as one who was pursued, immigrant, indigent, and had nothing. When he arrived there, he built his mosque and built chambers around it for his wives and companions. He himself used to live in that mud and baked clay chamber.

Those chambers were so small that even ten people standing beside each other could hardly fit in. After the death of the Prophet, when people came to offer prayers for him, a maximum of ten could squeeze in to face the coffin and offer the prayers.

His circumstances changed after reaching Medina. He became the head of a state, and funds were brought to him from all over that expanded state. Yet, his chamber did not change to become a huge house, nor did his simple furnishings change to become luxurious.

Prophet was the most generous of all people, the most patient, the most truthful, the trustworthiest, the most kind, and the best companion. Whoever saw him would be in awe of him; whoever associated with him would love him. He used to unite people together rather than make them shun each other; he was generous to everyone, known to be honorable among his people and he was granted authority over them. He used to say, "If a man is held by his folks as honorable, you, too, should honor him."

He used to always enquire about his companions. He distributed his attention fairly among those in his company, so much so that none of them would think that someone else was better than him. If someone kept his company and he had something, which he wanted, the Prophet would be patient with him until he himself would be the one to part. If anyone asked him for something, he would respond by giving it to him, or else he would give him sufficient assurances in its regard.

He used to say, "Respond to whoever asks you even with a little, or say something beautiful to him."And he also used to say, "The best of rulers is one who unites the disunited folks, and the worst is one who disunites those who are united."

Chapter 5:
Selected Sayings Of The Prophet Muhammad

Selected Sayings Of Prophet Muhammad
The teachings and the saying of an individual to a great extent reveal, just as his actions do, the true character and real nature of the individual. It is due to the majesty of the words of the Prophet, which is but a drop from the ocean of knowledge and wisdom of the Messenger of Allah, and his morality and the essence of his character, that these words and thousands like them have remained eternal since the Prophet first spoke them. They will continue to remain so forever.

Therefore the Muslims, who number more than one and a half billion, together with many others look upon these words and teachings as sources of inspiration, examples of wisdom and laws of vitality in all aspects of life. These masses are proud of adhering to some of them and endeavor in hope to implement those that they have not yet succeeded in doing.

On Supplication
The Apostle of God once said: 'shall I show you a weapon which will save you from your enemies and cause God's providence to flow upon you?' Those who

were present said: 'Yes!' He said: 'To call upon your Lord day and night, for the weapon of the believer is supplication.'1

He was once asked about the greatest name of God. He said: 'Each of the names of God is the greatest, so empty your heart of all but Him and call upon Him by any name you wish.'The Apostle of God said: 'Supplication is the essence of worship.'

He also said: 'Supplication is the weapon of the believer and the pillar of the faith and the light of heavens and earth.'4 He also said: 'A person will gain one of three things from supplication: either a sin will be forgiven, or a benefaction will be hastened to him, or a benefaction will be stored up for him.

He also said: 'Ask God of His bounty for He loves to be asked. The best of worship is to await the end of suffering.'6 By the "end of suffering"it means the suffering of mankind as a whole due to the widespread oppression that dominates the globe. This will end by the appearance of the awaited savior - the twelfth Imam from the descendent of the prophet Muhammad - Imam Mahdi peace be upon him. To await the appearance of Imam Mahdi is to ensure harmony with his teachings, which are the teachings of Islam. Thus this waiting is the best worship for it involves full compliance with the commands of Almighty Allah.

On Familial Bonds

It is related from Imam Ja'far al-Sadiq that: 'A man came
to the Prophet and said: 'O Apostle of God, whom
should I honour?'

He said: 'Your mother.'

The man said: 'And then whom?' He said: 'Your mother.'

The man said: 'And then whom?' The Prophet said:
'Your mother.'

The man said: 'And then whom?' The Prophet said:
'Your father.

The Apostle of God used to say: 'The angel Gabriel did
not stop enjoining upon me respect for women until I
thought that even divorce was not permissible except in
the case of proven adultery.

He also said: 'I advise those present from my nation and
those absent, and those who are in the loins of men and
the wombs of women, until the Day of Resurrection, to
maintain the bonds of kinship even if it means travelling
for a whole year, for that is a part of the religion.'9

A man once came to the Prophet and said: 'I have never
ever kissed one of my children.' When he had left the
Prophet said: 'This is a man who in my opinion deserves
to go to Hell.'

Once, the Apostle of God saw a man with two sons who kissed one of them and neglected the other. He said: 'Why have you not treated them both equally?'

A man asked the Apostle of God: 'What rights should a father expect from his child?' He said: 'He should not call his father by his name, and he should not walk in front of his father, and he should not sit down before his father does.'A man said: 'O Apostle of God, what are the rights of this son of mine?'

He said: 'You should give him a good name and a good education and enable him to gain good skills for good means of earning.'

On Good Morals And Conducts

The Prophet said: 'He, whose ethics are good, will be given by God the degree of one who continuously fasts and keeps vigil.'He also said: 'Nothing better than good ethics can be put in the balance scales of a person on the Day of Resurrection.' He said: 'The most beloved of you to me and the one who will sit closest to me on the Day of Resurrection is the best of you in ethics and the most humble of you.'

He said: 'Conducts are gifts from Almighty God. If God loves one of his servants He will give to him fine morals and conducts, but if he dislikes one of His servants he will give him foul manners.' Commenting on the outcome of one's conducts and ethics the Prophet declared: 'Adopt fine ethics, for it is inevitable that good

morals will end up in Paradise. Avoid bad conducts for it
is inevitable that bad ethics will end up in Hellfire.'

He said: 'With good ethics and conduct, a person will
reach the greatest of degrees and the noblest of stations
in the afterlife even if his worship was somewhat weak.'

He then said: 'With foul conduct and behaviour a person
will reach the lowest reaches of Hell.'
In the now famous and well known speech of Prophet
Muhammad that summarizes his entire mission and puts
it in perspective, he declared: 'Verily, I have been sent to
perfect the finest of morals.

Once he was told: 'There is a woman who fasts all day
and keeps vigil at night but she is ill mannered and
annoys her neighbours.' He said: 'There is nothing good
about her, she is destined for Hellfire.'

The Prophet said: 'Shall I tell you which of you from
amongst you is most like me?' They said: 'Yes, O
Apostle of God.' He said: 'The best of you in morals, and
the most pliant of you, and the one who honors his
relatives the most, and the one who has the strongest
love for his brothers in faith, and the one who is most
patient in the way of the truth, and he who is most in
control of his anger, and is most forgiving, and he who is
most just to himself in contentment and in anger.'

He said: 'The best of you are those whose morals are
best, whose houses receive frequent visitors, who
socialize by inviting and accepting invitations of others,

and whose furniture is worn out by having frequent visitors and guests.'

He said: 'If you meet with one another then meet with a greeting of 'peace' and a handshake. And when you disperse then disperse asking for forgiveness (for each other).'

He said: ' . . .You will never encompass the people with your wealth so greet them with a good countenance and a good smile.'26 The Prophet said: 'I urge you to adopt the finest of morals for Almighty God has sent me with them. Amongst the fine morals are that a man forgive those who have wronged him, and give to those that have withheld from him, and maintain ties with those who have cut off from him, and visit those who do not visit him.'

He also said: 'Shall I show you the best morals of this world and the next? ... That you maintain bonds with those who cut off from you, and give to those who withhold from you, and forgive those who have wronged you.'

He used to encourage: 'Be a good companion to those who accompany you and you will be a good Muslim.' He used to stress this matter to his followers in question form: 'Shall I show you the best morals of this world and the next? They eagerly responded, "Yes O Messenger of Allah!"So the Prophet replied: By spreading peace in the world.'

Aswad ibn Ashram relates: 'I said to the Apostle of God: 'Advise me.' He said: 'Do you own your hand?' I said: 'Yes.' He said: 'Do you own your tongue?' I said: 'Yes.' He said: 'Then do not extend your hand except to do good and do not say with your tongue anything that is not appropriate.'

It is related that the Commander of the Faithful Imam Ali said: 'A man asked to see the Apostle of God and said to him: 'O Apostle of God, advise me!' He said: 'I advise you to associate no partners with God even if you are cut into pieces and incinerated by fire, and do not dishonor your father and mother, and do not insult the people, and if you meet your Muslim brother then meet him with a nice smile...'

On Clemency

The Prophet said: 'The most clement of the people is he who flees from the ignorant people.'33 He also said: 'There are three things which if not found in a person that person's actions will not be complete: abstinence which protects him from disobedience to God, morals with which he interacts with the people, and clemency with which he repels the ignorance of the ignorant.'34 One day the Prophet asked his companions: 'Who amongst you is considered to be a champion?'

They said: 'The severe and powerful person who never compromises.' The Prophet replied: 'On the contrary, the true champion is a man who is struck by Satan in his heart until his anger intensifies and his blood boils but then he remembers God and by his clemency defeats his anger.'

On another occasion the Apostle of God said to his companions: 'Shall I inform you of the one amongst you who is most like me?' They said: 'Yes, O Apostle of God.' He said: ' ... the most patient of you in the way of the truth and the one most in control of his anger.'

The Prophet used to say: 'There are two draughts which are two of the most beloved ways to Almighty God: a draught of anger which is repelled by clemency and a draught of calamity which is repelled by patience.'

It is related that Imam Ali said: 'The Apostle of God said: 'My Lord has ordered me to act civilly with the people just as he has ordered me to perform the obligatory prayers.'

He also said: 'I have been sent as a center for clemency and as a mine for knowledge and as an abode for patience.'

Once a young man came to the Apostle of God and said to him: 'Do you give me permission to fornicate?' The Apostle of God's companions rebuked him and were rough with him; but the Prophet brought him near and said: 'Would you like it if others fornicated with your mother and your sisters and your aunts?' He said: 'No, O Apostle of God.' He said to him: 'All people feel the same way.' Then he put his blessed hand on his chest and

said: 'O God, forgive his sin and purify his heart and
protect his private parts.'

He also said: 'Allah favored the prophets over the rest of
his creation due to their extensive affability towards the
enemies of the religion of God and for their excellent
prudence for the sake of their brothers in God.'

On Being Conscious of Almighty God, the Apostle of
Allah said: 'Whoever fears God will live as a powerful
person and may travel in the land of his enemy in safety.'
He also said: 'Act according to what God has made
obligatory and you will be the most God-conscious of
the people.'

The Commander of the Faithful, Imam Ali, related: 'The
Apostle of God said: 'The most pious of the people is he
who speaks the truth whether it be in his favor or to his
detriment.'

The Apostle of God also said: 'Whoever wishes to be
the most pious of people then let him rely upon God.'

He also said: 'There are ten parts to worship, nine of
which are in lawful means of earning.'

He also said: 'Looking to your brother who you love for
the sake of God is an act of worship.'

It is related that Imam Ja'far al-Sadiq said: 'Whenever
the Apostle of God awoke from sleep he would fall
down and prostrate to God.'

In a tradition it has been said that the Prophet when
praying was as if he was a discarded robe.'

For ten years the Prophet stood in prayer on his toes
until his feet became raw and bloodied. His face became
yellow from keeping vigil at night until he was chided
for doing so when God said:

Taha, We did not send down the Qur'an upon you so
that you may become distressed (20:1-2).

In his advice the Prophet said to Abu Dharr: 'I enjoin
consciousness of God upon you for it is the summit of
all of your affairs.'
He also said: 'There is a trait which if adopted by a
person the whole of this world and the next will obey
him and he will profit by attaining Paradise.' He was
asked: 'And what is that O Apostle of God?'

He said: 'God consciousness (taqwa), for whoever
wishes to be the mightiest of people then let him develop
consciousness of God.' Then he recited God's words:

And whoever fears God, He will make for him a solution
and will provide for him from where he does not expect
(65:2-3).
On Forgiveness, Kindness And Mercy
It is related of the Prophet that he said: 'On the Day of
Resurrection a herald will call out: 'Whoever's reward is
with God then let him enter Paradise.' It will be asked:
'Whose reward is with God?' It will be answered: 'Those

who forgave the people, for they will enter Paradise
without being held to account.'

He would encourage mercy in general saying: 'Those
who show mercy will be shown mercy by The Merciful
One on the Day of Resurrection. Show mercy to those
on Earth and He who is in the heavens will show mercy
to you.'

Once al-Aqra Bin Habis saw the Apostle of God kissing
his grandsons al-Hasan and al-Husayn - the sons of
Imam Ali ibn Abu Talib. Al-Aqra Said: 'I have ten
children and I have never kissed any of them ever.' The
Apostle of God became angry and his color flushed and
he said to al-Aqra: 'He who shows no mercy shall not be
shown mercy. If you have torn all mercy from your own
heart then what can I do for you? He who shows no
mercy to the children or no respect to the elders is not
one of us.

He also said: 'Be to the orphans like a merciful father
and know that whatever you sow so shall you reap.
The noble Prophet said: 'When I was taken upon my
heavenly night journey I saw some people into whose
bellies fire was being cast and it was exiting from their
behinds. I said: 'Who are they, O Gabriel?' He said:
'They are -

those who consume the property of the orphans unjustly
(4:10).
He also said: 'I and the person who takes care of orphans
will be as close as these two fingers (and he indicated

with his index and middle fingers), in Paradise as long as he fears Almighty God.'

It is related that Abdullah ibn Masud narrated: 'The Apostle of God had said: 'Whoever gently strokes the head of an orphan will have a light on the Day of Resurrection for every hair that his hand passes over.'

Regarding forgiveness he said: 'Whoever forgives a wrong, God will give him honor in this world and the next.'
He also said: 'When anger raises its head dispel it with forgiveness, for a herald will call out on the Day of Resurrection: 'Let those whose reward is with God stand!' Then none shall stand but those who were forgiving. Have you not heard God's words? -

And whoever forgives and sets things to right, then his reward will be with God (42:40).
He also said: 'The virtue of us Ahl al-Bayt is to forgive those who wrong us, and to give to those who withhold from us.'

He also said: 'Forgiveness is most appropriate from the person who is most able to retaliate.' He also said: 'God loves kindness and assists those who are kind. So if you ride upon a lean beast then let it stop at its feeding stations. And if the land is arid then escape on it, and if the land is fertile then let it stop at its feeding stations.'

On Toiling And Earning That Which Is Lawful

The Prophet used to say: 'He who eats from what his
hand has toiled for will be counted amongst the Prophets
on the Day of Resurrection and will take the reward of
the Prophets.'

He also said: 'He who eats from what his hand has toiled
for will be looked upon by God with mercy, hence He
will never punish him.
He also said: 'He who eats from what his hand has toiled
for will pass over the sirat like lightning.'

He said: 'Seeking what is lawful is obligatory for every
Muslim man and woman.

He said: 'Whoever seeks in this world what is lawful to
keep himself from begging and to provide for his
dependents and to assist his neighbors will meet God on
the Day of Resurrection with a face radiant like the full
moon.

Whenever the Prophet liked the look of a man he would
ask: 'Does he have an occupation?' If he was told: 'No.'
He would say: 'He has gone down in my esteem.' He was
asked: 'And why is this O Apostle of God?' He said:
'Because the believer if he does not have a profession
will live at the expense of his religion.'

He also said: ' . . . but God loves a person who if he does
an act he does it well.'
He also said: 'He who toils for the sake of his dependents
is like he who strives in the cause of God.'

On Humility

The Apostle of God said once to his companions: 'Why is it that I do not see upon you the sweetness of worship?' They said: 'And what is the sweetness of worship?' He said: 'Humility.'

The Prophet was asked: 'What is humility?' He said: 'It is humbleness in prayer and that a person directs his entire heart towards his Lord.'
He also said: 'He who leaves off adornments for the sake of God and puts aside fine clothes out of humility to God and seeking His countenance, by rights God will store up for him the fine ubqari carpets of Paradise.'

He said in his testament to Abu Dharr, one of his most devout companions: 'Blessed is he who humbles himself for the sake of God and not due to some lack, and belittles himself but not due to destitutionm
He said: 'O Abu Dharr, he who leaves off wearing finery when he is able to do so out of humility to Almighty God will be enrobed by God with the robe of honor.'

He also said: 'When you see the humble ones from my nation then act humbly to them, and when you see the arrogant ones then act arrogantly towards them for this belittles and diminishes them.'

He said: 'It pleases me to see a man carrying something in his hand which he is bringing to please his family and which stops him from being arrogant.'

He said: 'A man should not humiliate himself.' He was
asked: 'O Apostle of God, and how does a man humiliate
himself?' He said: 'By exposing himself to that which he
cannot bear.'

One day the Apostle of God went on a journey with his
companions. He ordered them to cook a sheep. One man
said: 'I will slaughter it.' Another said: 'I will skin it.'
Another said: 'I will cook it.' The Apostle of God said: 'I
will go and fetch the firewood for you.' The companions
said: 'O Apostle of God may our fathers and mothers be
your sacrifice, do not tire yourself for we will do
everything for you.' The Apostle of God said: 'I know
that you will do so but Almighty God detests that a
person should be singled out amongst his companions.'
Then he went to collect the firewood for them.'

On The Reprehensibility Of Arrogance
The Prophet said: 'The tyrants and arrogant people will
be gathered in the Day of Resurrection in the form of
small ants to be stepped on by the people because of
their baseness in the eyes of Almighty God.'

He also said: 'He who considers himself to be
magnificent and swaggers in his gait will have the wrath
of Almighty God upon him when he meets Him.'

He also said: 'He who loves men to remain standing in
his presence then let him prepare his place in Hellfire.'84
256 He also said: 'He who drags his robe in the dust
haughtily will not be looked upon by God on the Day of
Resurrection.'

Once the Apostle of God passed by a group of people who had gathered and made a circle around a man so he said: 'Why have you gathered? They said: 'O Apostle of God, he is possessed and is having a fit so we have gathered around him.' He said: 'He is not possessed but he is afflicted.'

Then he said: 'Shall I tell you who one truly possessed is?' They said: 'Yes, O Apostle of God!' He said: 'He who swaggers in his gait and looks to his sides and moves his flanks with his shoulders. He hopes that God will give him Paradise but he disobeys Him. None are safe from his evils and none hope for any good from him. That is one possessed and this man is but afflicted.'

When he entered the House the Kabah on the day of the liberation of Mecca he said: 'Almighty God has done away with the pride and arrogance of the Arabs about their forefathers. All of you are from Adam, and Adam is from dust, and the most noble of you in the sight of God is the most pious of you.

He also said addressing Abu Dharr: 'Whoever dies and within his heart there is an atom's weight of arrogance will never experience the aroma of Paradise, except he who repents beforehand.' Then a man said: 'O Apostle of God, I am a great admirer of beauty. So much so that even the emblem of my whip and the straps of my sandals must be fine. Should this be a cause of concern?' He said: 'And how do you find your heart?' He said: 'I find it recognizing the truth and content with it.' The

Prophet said: 'This then is not arrogance but arrogance is to neglect the truth and to traverse it to something other than the truth, and to look to the people and think that there is no-one whose honor is like yours and whose blood is like yours.

It is related that Imam Ja'far al-Sadiq said: 'A poor man came to the Apostle of God when he was with a rich man. The rich man pulled up his robe and recoiled from the poor man. The Apostle of God said to him: 'What made you do what you did? Did you fear that his poverty would adhere to you or that your riches would adhere to him?' The rich man said: 'Now that you have said this then he can have half my wealth.' The Apostle of God said to the poor man: 'Do you accept?' The poor man said: 'No.' He said: 'Why?' The poor man said: 'I fear that I will become how he has become.

On Consultation

Imam Ja'far al-Sadiq relates that the Apostle of God was asked: 'O Apostle of God, what is prudence?' He said: 'To consult with those who are judicious and to follow their advice.' It is also related that Imam al-Sadiq said: 'Amongst that which the Apostle of God advised Imam Ali in his will was that he said: 'There is no support stronger than consultation and there is no intelligence like forward thinking.'

The Prophet said to the Commander of the Faithful: 'O Ali, do not consult with a cowardly person for he will make the solution very limited. And do not consult with

a miserly person for he will bring you short of your goal.
And do not consult with a greedy person for he will
make evil appear beautiful to you...'

He also said: 'Consulting with an intelligent person of
good counsel is good sense and good fortune and
success from God. If the intelligent person of good
counsel gives his opinion then do not oppose it for the
consequence of this is perdition.' It is also related that
the Prophet said: 'Whenever a man consults with another
he will be guided to good sense.'

It is related that Imam Ali said: 'The Apostle of God
said: 'Whoever is consulted by his brother in faith and he
does not give him sincere counsel then God will take
away his intelligence.'

On Generosity
The Apostle of God said: 'Generosity is a tree in
Paradise whose branches stretch down to this world.
Whoever is generous has taken hold of one of these
branches and this branch will lead him to Paradise.'96
The Prophet said to Odayy, son of Hatim al-Tai: 'Your
father has been spared the severe punishment because of
the generosity of his soul.'

Jarir ibn Abdullah relates: 'When the Prophet's mission
to teach Islam began and I came to pledge my allegiance
to him, he asked: 'O Jarir, for what reason have you
come?' I said: 'I have come to enter Islam at your hands
O Apostle of God.' Then he threw his cloak over me, and

turned to his companions to say: 'When the nobles of any
people come to you then honor them.

On Discouraging Miserliness
The Apostle of God said: 'The people who have least
peace of mind are the misers.

He asked his companions once: 'What is your definition
of a vagabond?' They said: 'A man who has no wealth.'
He said: 'No, the true vagabond is he who does not give
away anything of his wealth in order to seek his reward
from God even though he would be leaving a lot of
wealth behind him.'

He also said: 'Surely God hates one who was miserly all
his life and becomes generous near the time of his
death.'He also said: 'Never was wealth diminished by
almsgiving, so give freely and do not be miserly.'

He also said: 'God has some servants whom He has
favored with His blessings and He will continue to do so
as long as they spread them amongst the people. If they
withhold them though then God will divert His blessings
from them to others.'

He also said: 'Whoever refuses to give out of his wealth
to good people out of choice, God will divert his wealth
to evil people by force.'
Imam Ja'far al-Sadiq said: 'The Apostle of God never
ever refused to give to one who asked from him. If he
had something with him he would give him it and if he
did not then he would say: 'God will provide it.'

Once the Apostle of God went to al-Jaranah, a place between Mecca and al-Taif. There he divided up the wealth that had been taken as spoils after the battle of Hunayn. The people began to ask more from him and he gave to them until he was forced to retreat to a tree. The people took his cloak and scratched his back so that they could pull him away from the tree and all the while they kept asking him for the wealth. He said: 'O people, give me back my cloak. I swear that if I had sheep to the number of trees of Tuhamah, I would divide them amongst you; then you would not see me as cowardly or miserly.'

He also said: 'The one least like me amongst you is the miserly, the foul-mouthed and the indecent.'
He also said: 'The miser is far from God and far from the people, far from Paradise and near to Hellfire.'

On Fulfilling Promises

The Apostle of God said: 'Whoever believes in God and the Last Day should fulfil his promises.'

He also said: 'He who keeps not his promise has no faith.'
Imam Ja'far al-Sadiq relates: 'The Apostle of God made an appointment to meet a man at al-Sakhrah and said to him: 'I will wait for you here until you come.' The sun's heat became severe and his companions said to him: 'O Apostle of God, if only you were to move into the shade.' He said: 'I promised to meet him here, and if he

does not come then it will be against him on the Day of
Gathering.'

It is narrated that Ibn Abi al-Hamsa al-Amiri said: 'It was
before the advent of the mission of the Apostle of God
when I made an appointment with him to meet at a
certain place but I forgot about it for two days. On the
third day I went to the place and I found him there, and
the Apostle of God said: 'Young man you have caused
me hardship for I have been here for three days waiting
for you.'

On Patience And Bearing Hardships
The Prophet said: 'Succor comes with patience, relief
comes with trouble and ease comes with difficulty.'

He also said: 'Patience is a veil from troubles and an aid
against misfortunes.'
He also said: 'Patience is the best vehicle. Never did God
provide any of his servants anything better or vaster than
patience.'
He used to say: 'Faith is composed of two parts: one part
patience and one part gratitude.'

On Almsgiving

The Apostle of God said: 'Verily, the One God, besides
whom there is no god but He, because of almsgiving
repels disease and disaster and fire and drowning and the
collapse of buildings and insanity . . . (and he went on to
mention seventy types of evil.)'

The Prophet was asked: 'What is the best kind of
almsgiving?' He said: 'To give alms when you are in
good health, covet your wealth, hope to live on and you
fear poverty. Do not wait until your soul reaches your
throat.'

The Apostle of God was asked: 'What is the best kind of
almsgiving?' He said: 'To give to one of your relatives
who has enmity for you.'

He also said: 'The best kind of alms is the alms of the
tongue.' He was asked: 'O Apostle of God, and what is
the alms of the tongue?' He said: 'To intercede to free a
prisoner or to prevent bloodshed or to bring something
desirable to your brother or repel something detestable
from him.'

On Truthfulness

It is related that the Apostle of God said: 'The closest of
you to me tomorrow when we stand before God is he
who is most truthful in speech.'
He also said: 'The adornment of speech is truthfulness.'

He also said: 'Truthfulness is blessed and untruthfulness
is accursed.

He also said: 'The liar only lies because of an inferiority
in his own self.'

He also said: 'Do your utmost to avoid lies for lies invite vice and criminality, and vice and criminality lead to Hellfire.'

He also said: 'Among the greatest sins (is) the lying tongue.'

He also said: 'Too much lying takes away the good aura of a person.'

He also said: 'Lying is one of the doors of hypocrisy.

He also said: 'Telling lies diminishes providence.'

He was once asked: 'Can a believer be a coward?' He said: 'Yes.'

He was asked: 'Can he be miserly?' He said: 'Yes.' He was asked: 'Can he be a liar?' He said: 'No.'131 He said: 'Woe betide those who tell stories and lie in order to get people to laugh. Woe betide them, woe betide them.'

On Abstinence

The Apostle of God said: 'O people, this worldly life is a place of grief and is not a place of joy. It is a place of crookedness and is not a place of straightforwardness. Whoever recognizes this will not feel joy at the achievement of some hope or feel grief at wretchedness.

He said: 'This worldly life is transient. Whatever comes to you in your favor comes despite your incapacity. And whatever of it is against you, you will not be able to repel it with your power. He who has no hope in that which has passed him by will find repose for his body. He who is content with that which God has decreed for him will find happiness.'

He also said: 'If love of worldly things dwells in the heart of a person he will be afflicted by three things: endless toil, poverty from which he will never be free, and expectations which will never be realized.'

In his caution to his companion he said: 'O Abu Dharr, this world occupies people's hearts and bodies. Almighty God will ask us about how we luxuriated in that which he has made lawful, so what about that which he has made unlawful.'

The Prophet also said: 'Almighty God revealed to this world saying: 'make weary those who serve you and serve those who refuse you.'

He said: 'Do not curse this world for it is a good place for the believer: in the world he may achieve what is good and through it he may be delivered from what is evil. If a person says: 'May God curse the world.' The world says: 'May God curse he who has most disobeyed his Lord.'

The Prophet said: 'How can anyone work for the afterlife if his desire for this world is not cut off or his lust for it is not overcome.' He also said: 'Think often of death, for

whoever thinks often of death will surely abstain from
the things of this world.'

He said: 'O Abu Dharr, Whenever a person abstains from
this world God causes wisdom to grow in his heart and
be spoken from his tongue. Then He gives him insights
into the faults of the world and its malady and its
antidote and He takes him out of the world in safety to
the abode of peace.'

He advised Abu Dharr: 'O Abu Dharr, if you see that
your brother has abstained from this world then listen to
him for he will dispense wisdom.'The Prophet declared:
'Whoever abstains from this world will find calamities to
be insignificant.'

He also said: 'Desire for worldly things increases worry
and grief whereas abstinence from worldly things gives
repose to the heart and the body.'

Once one of the angels came to the Apostle of God and
said: 'O Muhammad, your Lord conveys you a greeting
of peace and says: 'If you wish I will fill for you the
valleys of Mecca with gold.'

The Prophet raised his head to the heavens and said: 'O
Lord, if I eat my fill one day I will praise you, and if I go
hungry the next day I will ask from you.' The Prophet
said to his companion about backbiting advising him: 'O
Abu Dharr, do your utmost to avoid backbiting, for it is
worse than adultery.' Abu Dharr said: 'O Apostle of God,
how is this so?'

The Prophet replied: 'This is so because if a man commits adultery and then repents to God, God will accept his repentance. But backbiting will not be forgiven until the person who has been spoken against gives forgiveness.'

The Prophet said to his companions: 'Shall I tell you who is the worst amongst you?' They said: 'Yes, O Apostle of God.' He said: 'Those who go about slandering and try to cause splits between loved ones and who seek faults in the innocent.The Prophet also said: 'The worst of the people is he who takes his brother to the court of the authorities whereby he destroys himself, his brother and the ruler.'

He also said to his companions: 'Shall I tell you who is the least like me?' They said: 'Yes, O Apostle of God.' He said: 'The miserly, the foul-mouthed, and the indecent.'He also said in his sermon at the farewell pilgrimage: 'Your blood and your property and your honors are sacred just as this day is sacred and this month is sacred.'

He also said: 'To sit in the mosque awaiting the time of prayer is an act of worship as long as the person does not backbite.'

On Justice

The Prophet said: 'No nation which does not firmly take the rights of the weak from the strong will ever be venerated.' He also said: 'The best of actions are: treating people fairly, and helping out your brother in the name of Lord, and remembrance of God in all circumstances.'

The Prophet Muhammad stated: 'An hour's justice is better than seventy years of worship, fasting during the day and keeping vigil during the night. An hour's injustice in ruling is worse and more serious in the sight of God than sixty years of sin.'

The Prophet also said: 'The most just of the people is one who likes for the people to have what he likes for himself, and detests for the people what he detests for himself.'

He said: 'What you dislike for yourself, you should dislike for others and what you like for yourself you should like for others. Then you will be just in your rule and equal in your justice, beloved of the people of the heavens and win the devotion of hearts of the people of the earth.'

He said: 'Beware of wronging for it is the darkness of the Day of Resurrection.'

He also said: 'If a mountain were to transgress against another mountain, God would turn the transgressor into dust.' He used to say: 'Transgression is the evil which has the swiftest of punishments.'

He said: 'He who takes from the wrongdoer and gives to the wronged will be in my company in Paradise.' He

said: 'On the day of Resurrection a herald will call out:
'Where are the oppressors and those who aided them?
Who poured ink for them? Who tied a bag for them?
Who extended a hand to help them? Herded them up
with the oppressors!'

He also said: 'The prayer of the person wronged is
answered even if it is from a non-practicing individual
who fears for himself.'He said: 'Whoever kills a non-
Muslim person under the protection of the Islamic state
will be forbidden Paradise whose perfume can be smelt
from twelve years journey away.'

He said: 'In Hellfire I saw the owner of a cat, which was
mauling her in front and behind. This was because she
used to tie it up and did not feed it or let it loose to eat
from the vermin of the earth.'

Words Of Light

The Prophet Muhammad said: 'All will be well with my
nation as long as they love one another, give gifts to one
another, fulfil their trusts, avoid that which is unlawful,
honor the guest, establish the prayer, and pay the
statutory alms. If they do not do this then they will be
afflicted by drought and famine.'

He said: 'All will be well with this nation under the hand
of God and in His protection as long as the reciters of the
Qur'an do not aid the rulers, and the righteous do not
praise the miscreants, and the good people do not assist

the evil ones. If they do this then God will lift His hand
from them and will place tyrants to rule over them ...'

He also said: 'There are three things I fear for my nation:
obedience to greed, following of lusts and desires, and
leaders who are astray.'
He said: 'Hope is a mercy for my nation. Were it not for
hope, no mother would ever feed her child and no
gardener would ever plant a tree. Once he said to his
companions: 'Shall I inform you of the worst of people?'

Those with him said: 'Yes, O Apostle of God.' He said:
'He who loathes the people and who is loathed by the
people.'

Then he said: 'Shall I inform you of something worse
than him?' They said: 'Yes, O Apostle of God.' He said:
'He who does not help another who has fallen and does
not accept another's apology and does not forgive a
wrong.'

Then he said: 'Shall I inform you of something worse
than him?' They said: 'Yes, O Apostle of God.' He said:
'He from whom none is safe from his evil and from
whom none expect any good.'1

He also said: 'Shall I inform you of the worst of your
men?' They said: 'Yes, O Apostle of God.' He said:
'Among the worst of your men is the slanderer, the
audacious transgressor, the obscene person who eats
alone and refuses to help others. He beats his servants
and forces his dependents to seek help elsewhere.'

The Apostle of God said to the Commander of the Faithful, Imam Ali: 'Say: 'O God, do not let me be in need of the worst of your creation!' The Commander of the Faithful said: 'O Apostle of God, and who is the worst of God's creation?'

He said: 'Those who when they are given refuse to give, and if they are refused something they would criticize or slander.'The Prophet was asked: 'Who are the worst of people?' He said: 'The corrupt savants.' The Apostle of God was asked: 'Who is your true nation?'

He said: 'Those who are with the truth though they may only be ten people.' He also said: 'The best of my nation are those who are most abstinent in the things of this world and who are most desirous of the next world.'

He also said: 'The best of my nation is one who spends his youth in obedience to God and weans himself off the pleasures of this world and is focused on the next life. His reward with God will be the highest stations in Paradise.'

He also said: 'Blessed is he who spends what he has earned without disobeying God, and keeps the company of the people of knowledge and wisdom and mixes with the underlings and the poor. Blessed is he whose self has been subdued and whose temperament is good and whose inner heart is virtuous and who keeps his worst aspects away from the people. Blessed is he who gives away his surplus wealth and holds back from what is superfluous in speech and who confines himself to Prophetic practices and does not go beyond them to innovations.

He also said: 'He who is not trustworthy has no faith.' Once Abu Ayyub Khalid ibn Zayd came to the Apostle of God and said: 'O Apostle of God, advise me and be brief so that I may remember what you say.' He said: 'I advise you to do five things: do not concern yourself with what is in the hands of others for that is riches, and do not be greedy for that is poverty itself, and pray each prayer as if it was your last, and avoid that which is regrettable, and love for your brother what you love for yourself.'

He also said: 'If you see one of the gardens of Paradise then go there and graze.' They said: 'O Apostle of God, and what is the garden of Paradise?'

He said: 'The gatherings of the believers.

He said in his advice to Abu Dharr: 'O Abu Dharr, do not procrastinate for you only have one day and you are not for what comes after it. If tomorrow were to be for you then be on the morrow as you were today. And if no tomorrow comes then you will not regret wasting your day.' 'O Abu Dharr, how often does someone greet a new day but does not live to see its end, and how often does someone await the morning and he does not see it.'

'O Abu Dharr, were you to look at your lifespan and its fate you would loathe desire and its delusions.'

'O Abu Dharr, Be in this world as if you are a stranger,
or as a passer by, and count yourself amongst the people
of the graves. 'O Abu Dharr, when morning comes do
not speak to yourself of the evening, and when evening
comes do not speak to yourself of the morning. Take
advantage of your health before you are ill, and your life
before your death, for you do not know what your name
will be on the morrow i.e. whether you are going to be
amongst the fortunate or the unfortunate.'

Abu Dharr also relates: 'The Apostle of God advised me
to do seven things: he advised me to look to those who
are below me and not to look to those who are above me.
He advised me to love the paupers and to be near to
them. He advised me to speak the truth even if it is
bitter. He advised me to maintain bonds with my kin
even if they turn away from me. He advised me not to
fear any blame in the way of God. He advised me to say
often: 'There is no strength or power except through God
The Exalted, The Magnificent', for these are the jewels
of Paradise.'

It is related that a man came to the Prophet and said: 'O
Apostle of God, advise me.' The Prophet said: 'Do you
seek advice so that I may advise you?' He said this three
times and each time the man said: 'Yes, O Apostle of
God.'

So the Apostle of God said to him: 'I advise that when
you intend to do something then think out its
consequences. If it is sensible then carry it out and if not

then refrain from it. Once a man said to the Apostle of God: 'Advise me!' He said: 'Have shame in front of God just as you have shame in front of a righteous man from your people.'

Among his advice to Muadh ibn Jabal, when he sent him as his representative to the Yemen, he said: 'I advise you to be conscious of God, and to be truthful in speech, and to honor pledges, and to fulfil trusts, and not to betray, and to be softly spoken, and to promote peace, and to protect refugees, and show mercy to the orphans, and to control your anger, and to act well, and to cut short your hopes, and to have love for the next world, and to fear the reckoning, and to adhere to faith to the last moment of your life, and to study the Qur'an, and to lower your wing i.e. be kind to others ...'

The Prophet Muhammad said: 'The best of combat is to combat with one's self that is between one's flanks.'

Chapter 6:
Prophet Muhammad As Seen By Western Thinkers

The religion of Muhammad will be the system upon which peace and contentment will be founded. The world today is in dire need of a man like Muhammad to solve its complex problems.
Sir George Bernard-Shaw
****

The following are some observations on the Prophet Muhammad, by well-acknowledged Western scholars and thinkers of modern times:

There is no doubt that the Prophet Muhammad was a great reformer who did a magnificent service to human society. It is honor enough to say that he guided a whole nation to the light of truth and caused it to incline towards stability and peace and to prefer an ascetic lifestyle. He prevented it from shedding blood and presenting human sacrifices. He opened up for it the way of prosperity and civic living. This is a tremendous achievement, which can only be undertaken by a powerful personality. A man like this is worthy of respect and honor.

The renowned Russian writer Count Leo Nikolayevich
Tolstoi

I wanted to know the best of the life of one who holds
today an undisputed sway over the hearts of millions of
mankind.... I became more than ever convinced that it
was not the sword that won a place for Islam in those
days in the scheme of life. It was the rigid simplicity, the
utter self- effacement of the Prophet the scrupulous
regard for pledges, his intense devotion to his friends
and followers, his intrepidity, his fearlessness, his
absolute trust in God and in his own mission. These and
not the sword carried everything before them and
surmounted every obstacle. When I closed the second
volume (of the Prophet's biography), I was sorry there
was not more for me to read of that great life.
Mahatma Gandhi, statement published in 'Young India'
1924

My choice of Muhammad (570 CE - 630 CE) to lead the
list of the world's most influential persons may surprise
some readers and may be questioned by others, but he
was the only man in history who was supremely
successful on both the secular and religious level. ...It is
probable that the relative influence of Muhammad on
Islam has been larger than the combined influence of
Jesus Christ and St. Paul on Christianity. ...It is this
unparalleled combination of secular and religious
influence which I feel entitles Muhammad to be
considered the most influential single figure in human
history.

Michael H. Hart, "The 100: A Ranking of the Most
Influential Persons in History", New York, 1987.

No other religion in history spread so rapidly as Islam.
The West has widely believed that this surge of religion
was made possible by the sword. But no modern scholar
accepts this idea, and the Qur'an is explicit in the
support of the freedom of conscience.
James Michener 'Islam: The Misunderstood Religion'
Reader's Digest, May 1955, pp. 68-70

I hold the religion of Muhammad in the highest esteem
for its astounding vitality. It seems to me to be the only
religion which is equipped to suit the changing faces of
life and which is appropriate for all ages. I have studied
the life of this amazing man and I believe that he
deserves to be called the savior of the human race.

If any religion had the chance of ruling over England,
nay Europe within the next hundred years, it could be
Islam. I believe that if a man like him were to assume the
dictatorship of the modern world he would succeed in
solving its problems in a way that would bring it the
much needed peace and happiness: I have prophesied
about the faith of Muhammad that it would be acceptable
to the Europe of tomorrow as it is beginning to be
acceptable to the Europe of today."
Sir George Bernard Shaw 'The Genuine Islam' Vol. 1,
No. 8,

Europe has begun now to sense the wisdom of
Muhammad and has developed a passion for his religion.

It will also come to exonerate Islamic doctrine from all
the false accusations laid at its door by Europeans in the
Middle Ages. The religion of Muhammad will be the
system upon which peace and contentment will be
founded. From his Philosophy, Europe will derive the
solution to perplexities, problems and complexities . . .
Many of my fellow countrymen and other Europeans
venerate the teachings of Islam. Hence I confirm my
prophecy by saying that the first stirrings of the age of
European Islam are near, this is inevitable.

Yes, the world today is in dire need of a man like
Muhammad to solve its complex problems.

Muhammad was abstemious and simple in his abode, his
food and his drink and his clothing and in the rest of his
life and conditions. His food consisted mainly of bread
with dates and water. He often mended his own clothes.
What could be more honorable than this?

Hail Muhammad the Prophet of rough clothing and food,
who strived, was active during the day and awake during
the night and persistent in promoting the religion of
Allah. He was not one to covet that which lesser men
covet such as rank, empire and power. He is in truth the
Prophet of the sublime morals.

A silent great soul - one that who could not but be
earnest, he was to kindle the world as the Maker of the
world had ordered so. The lies which well-meaning zeal
has heaped round this man [Muhammad] are disgraceful
to us only.

The English philosopher Thomas Carlyle 'Heroes, Hero Worship and the Heroic in History' 1840

Never has a man set for himself, voluntarily or involuntarily, a more sublime aim, since this aim was superhuman; to subvert superstitions which had been imposed between man and his Creator, to render God unto man and man unto God; to restore the rational and sacred idea of divinity amidst the chaos of the material and disfigured gods of idolatry, then existing. Never has a man undertaken a work so far beyond human power with so feeble means, for he (Muhammad) had in the conception as well as in the execution of such a great design, no other instrument than himself and no other aid except a handful of men living in a corner of the desert. Finally, never has a man accomplished such a huge and lasting revolution in the world, because in less than two centuries after its appearance, Islam, in faith and in arms, reigned over the whole of Arabia, and conquered, in God's name, Persia, Western India, Abyssinia, Syria, Egypt, all the known continent of Northern Africa, Spain, etc.

If greatness of purpose, smallness of means, and astounding results are the three criteria of human genius, who could dare to compare any great man in modern history with Muhammad? The most famous men have created arms, laws and empires only. They founded, if anything at all, no more than material powers which often crumbled before their eyes. This man moved not only armies, legislations, empires, peoples and dynasties, but millions of men in one-third of the then inhabited world; and more than that, he moved the altars, the gods, the religions, the ideas, the beliefs and souls . . . his forbearance in victory, his ambition, which was entirely devoted to one idea and in no manner striving for an empire; his endless prayers, his mystic conversations with God, his death and his triumph after death; all these attest not to an imposture but to a firm conviction which gave him the power to restore a dogma. This dogma was twofold, the unity of God and the immateriality of God - the former telling what God is, the latter what God is not.

Philosopher, Orator, Apostle, Legislator, Warrior, Conqueror of Ideas, Restorer of Rational beliefs... The Founder of twenty terrestrial empires and of one Spiritual Empire - that is Muhammad. As regards all standards by which human greatness may be measured, we may ask, is there any man greater than he? Alphonse de La Martaine 'Historie de la Turquie', v. ii, Paris, 1854

His simple eloquence, rendered impressive by the expression of a countenance wherein awfulness of majesty was tempered by an amiable sweetness, excited emotions of veneration and love; and he was gifted with that authoritative air of genius which alike influences the learned and commands the illiterate. As a friend and a parent, he exhibited the softest feelings of our nature . . . With all that simplicity which is so natural to a great mind, he performed the humbler offices whose homeliness it would be idle to conceal with pompous diction; even while Lord of Arabia, he mended his own

shoes and coarse woolen garments, milked the ewes,
swept the hearth, and kindled the fire, dates and water
were his usual fare, and milk and honey his luxuries.
When he travelled he divided his morsel with his
servant.
John Davenport "An Apology for Mohammed and the
Koran"London 1869

Head of the State as well as the Church, he was Caesar
and Pope in one; but he was Pope without Pope's
pretensions, and Caesar without the legions of Caesar:
without a standing army, without a bodyguard, without a
palace, without a fixed revenue. if ever any man had the
right to say that he ruled by the divine right, it was
Mohammad, for he had all the power without its
instruments and without its supports. He cared not for
the dressings of power. The simplicity of his private life
was in keeping with his public life.

In Mohammedanism everything is different here. Instead
of the shadowy and the mysterious, we have history....
We know of the external history of Muhammad.... while
for his internal history after his mission had been
proclaimed, we have a book absolutely unique in its
origin, in its preservation.... on the Substantial authority
of which no one has ever been able to cast a serious
doubt.
Reverend Bosworth Smith "Mohammed and
Mohammedanism"London 1874

The good sense of Mohammed despised the pomp of
royalty. The Apostle of God submitted to the menial

offices of the family; he kindled the fire; swept the floor; milked the ewes; and mended with his own hands his shoes and garments.

Mohammed - was distinguished by the beauty of his person that was an outward gift, which is seldom despised, except by those to whom it has been refused. Before he spoke, the orator engaged on his side the affections whether of a public or a private audience. They applauded his commanding presence, his majestic aspect, his piercing eye, his gracious smile, his flowing beard, his countenance, which painted every sensation of his soul, and the gestures that enforced each expression of the tongue. In the familiar offices of life, he scrupulously adhered to the grave and ceremonious politeness of his country; his respectful attention to the rich and powerful was dignified by his condescension and affability to the poorest citizen of Mecca; his memory was capacious and retentive, his wit easy and social, his imagination sublime, his judgement clear, rapid and decisive. He possessed the courage both of thought and action; bears the stamp of an original and superior genius.
Edward Gibbon "Decline and Fall of the Roman Empire"1823

History makes it clear, however, that the legend of fanatical Muslims sweeping through the world and forcing Islam at the point of sword upon conquered races is one of the most fantastically absurd myths that historians have ever repeated.
De Lacy O'Leary 'Islam at the Crossroads' London, 1923

Incidentally these well-established facts dispose of the idea so widely fostered in Christian writings that the Muslims, wherever they went, forced people to accept Islam at the point of the sword.
Lawrence E. Browne 'The Prospects of Islam' 1944

To suppose Muhammad an impostor raises more problems that it solves. Moreover, none of the great figures of history is so poorly appreciated in the West as Muhammad.... Thus, not merely must we credit Muhammad with essential honesty and integrity of purpose, if we are to understand him at all. If we are to correct the errors we have inherited from the past, we must not forget that the conclusive proof is a much stricter requirement than a show of plausibility, and in a matter such as this, it is only to be attained with difficulty.
W. Montgomery Watt 'Muhammad at Mecca' Oxford, 1953

Muhammad, the Messenger of Islam, exhibited for most of his life if not all of his life a striking moderateness. His final victory points to a greatness of character rarely to be found in history. He ordered his army to give quarter to the old and the weak, the children and the women, and warned them against destroying houses or pillaging or cutting down fruiting trees. He ordered them not to draw their swords except in dire need. It is even said that he used to rebuke some of his generals and physically put right their mistakes.
Emil Dirmargen, Orientalist, "The Life of Muhammad"

Muhammad, the Messenger of Allah was courageous in fighting battles himself giving strength and endurance to the hearts of those who were weaker. He was merciful with the weak, and would give refuge to a great number of the needy in his house. Although he maintained a reverential aura, he had a plain manner about him with no affectation whatsoever. He was cheerful and easy to deal with and with an even temper not easily angered by inquisitive people and always had a smile on his face.

There is no doubt that he had many traits which made him attractive to the people of his time, but he had conveyed to those people a sublime example in religion and morals, and transcended the old notions under which they were suffering. When he had gathered them as one body under the banner of this sublime example, he made from them a power, which later shook the very foundations of the Ancient world.
Florandes & Marseille - The Eastern World

Muhammad, the messenger of Islam possessed noble traits such as gentleness, bravery, and the noblest of morals. A person was not able to evaluate him without being affected by these attributes. Muhammad bore the enmity of his family and tribe for years without losing determination or strength. His nobility was such that he would never be the first to withdraw his hand from one who shook hands with him even from a child and he would never pass by a group of people men or children without giving a greeting of peace, all the while smiling

sweetly and with beautiful words which would enchant
he who heard them and win his heart.
The English Orientalist Hollen Paul

The Qur'an is a splendid humanistic document, which
explains in detail the secret of the behaviour of
Muhammad in all the events of his life. We even find
therein an additional subject matter through which we
are able to follow the progress of Islam from its
inception and appearance in its early history. We do not
find the like in Buddhism or Christianity or any of the
other ancient religions. These are the unique features of
Islam and they confirm and prove that it is the complete
religion for humanity and that it is the religion of the
future.
The Scottish Orientalist Ronald A. Nicholson

The greatest success of Mohammad's life was affected
by sheer moral force. It is not the propagation but the
permanency of his religion that deserves our wonder; the
same pure and perfect impression, which he engraved at
Mecca and Medina is preserved after the revolutions of
twelve centuries by the Indian, the African and the
Turkish proselytes of the Koran....

The Mohammedans have uniformly withstood the
temptation of reducing the object of their faith and
devotion to a level with the senses and imagination of
man. 'I believe in One God and Mohammad the Apostle
of God' is the simple and invariable profession of Islam.
The intellectual image of the Deity has never been
degraded by any visible idol; the honors of the prophet

have never transgressed the measure of human virtue,
and his living precepts have restrained the gratitude of
his disciples within the bounds of reason and religion.
Edward Gibbon & Simon Oakley 'History of the Saracen
Empire' London, 1870

Islam is a religion that is essentially rationalistic in the
widest sense of this term considered etymologically and
historically.... the teachings of the Prophet, the Qur'an
has invariably kept its place as the fundamental starting
point, and the dogma of unity of God has always been
proclaimed therein with a grandeur a majesty, an
invariable purity and with a note of sure conviction,
which it is hard to find surpassed outside the pale of
Islam.... A creed so precise, so stripped of all theological
complexities and consequently so accessible to the
ordinary understanding might be expected to possess and
does indeed possess a marvelous power of winning its
way into the consciences of men.
T. W. Arnold 'The Preaching of Islam' London 1913

Four years after the death of Justinian, A.D. 569, was
born in Mecca, in Arabia, the man who, of all men, has
exercised the greatest influence upon the human race...
To be the religious head of many empires, to guide the
daily life of one-third of the human race, may perhaps
justify the title of a Messenger of God.
Dr. William Draper 'History of Intellectual Development
of Europe'

The Arabian Prophet had powerful and strong morals
and a personality, which weighed up, examined, and

tested every step he took in his life. There is no fault in his character whatsoever. Given that we are in need of a complete paradigm to fulfil our needs in life, the personality of Muhammad the Holy Prophet fulfils this need. It is the mirror, which reflects for us lofty reasoning, magnanimity, nobility, bravery, patience, kindness, humility, forgiveness, humbleness and modesty and all the essential morals of which humanitarianism. We see this present in the personality of the Prophet Muhammad in glowing colors.
Lord Hadleigh

I thought and prayed for forty years so that I might arrive at the truth. I must confess that my visit to the Islamic east filled me with respect for the serene [Islamic] faith, which induces one to worship God all throughout one's life not just on Sundays. I am eternally grateful to God that he has guided me to Islam, which has become a firm reality in my heart and has allowed me to attain happiness and tranquility, which previously were not attainable. I was in a dark cavern, then Islam took me out into an expansive land illuminated by the Sun and I began to smell the pure fresh sea air.

Chapter 7
Conclusion

There are many such incidents which all point out to the Prophet Muhammad's wide popularity, great manners, humility, loyalty and wise government - the like of which history had never known before him nor knew after him.

Hence rulers should use him as their role model, if they wish to be near to Allah and to win the best of the Hereafter. Imam Ali has said, "Whoever seeks a role model, let the Prophet be his role model; otherwise, he shall have no safeguard against perdition."